W9-BEQ-049

CHICAGO
THE GLAMOUR YEARS (1919-1941)

CHICAGO
THE GLAMOUR YEARS (1919-1941)

**THOMAS G AYLESWORTH
& VIRGINIA L AYLESWORTH**

GALLERY BOOKS
An imprint of W.H. Smith Publishers Inc.
112 Madison Avenue
New York, New York 10016

A Bison Book

Published by Gallery Books
A Division of W H Smith Publishers Inc.
112 Madison Avenue
New York, New York 10016

Produced by
Bison Books Corp.
17 Sherwood Place
Greenwich, CT 06830

Copyright ⓒ1986 Bison Books Corp.

All rights reserved. No part of this book may be reproduced or
transmitted in any form or by any means without written
permission from the Publisher.

ISBN 0-8317-1254-6

Printed in Hong Kong

1   2   3   4   5   6   7   8   9   10

CONTENTS

PRELUDE

Chicago – Chicago. Breathe the name of this mid-continent metropolis to most Americans and thoughts lightly turn to stockyards and sausage, railroads and ribs, wind, cold, conventions and Al Capone. But conjure instead a crescent of comfortable beaches, green playing fields, colorful marinas bounded by an azure inland sea and backdropped by a forest of gleaming skyscrapers.

Think of one of the world's best symphony orchestras, the nation's most vibrant regional theater, superb museums containing timeless masterpieces and innovative, interactive exhibits, intimate clubs where jazz remains cool and hot. Savor restaurants serving high, middle and low cuisine from the best regional kitchens of the five continents' four corners.

Add a dizzying maze of factories set among impacted neighborhoods. Web it together with the world's busiest airport, a noisy, friendly subway on stilts and booming arteries across an endless grid of streets stretching to the edge of the Great Prairie.

Left: A 1929 photograph shows the tablet indicating the site of the first Chicago home, built in 1779.

Page 1: The Edgewater Beach Hotel's trellis-patterned Marine Dining Room in the 1920s.

Pages 2 – 3: An aerial view of the city in the 1930s.

Previous pages: The Chicago stockyards in 1861.

Opposite: Wacker Drive, along the Chicago River, is a doubledeck thorough-fare.

Below: An engraving of a Chicago scene in the 1850s. The Water Tower (center) was the only building in the area to survive the Great Chicago Fire.

This sprawling complexity, this concentration of contradictions, this place of ceaseless movement, this glory and grime – this is Chicago, the most real American city in all of America.

The Queen City of these open flatlands, Chicago – the metropolis of the Midwest – is not an old city like Boston, New York or St Augustine. And unlike Boston, Philadelphia, New York or Washington, the atmosphere of England and the Colonial and Federal Periods does not dominate. Unlike Miami, Chicago is for hard work, hard winters, grit. Unlike Los Angeles, Chicago is, in fact, a city, where hordes of people roam a true downtown, rub elbows, ride a real subway, vie for cabs and do other things that knit them into a genuine urban community.

True, Chicago is not an old city. But long before the first white settlers arrived, the Chicago area was important to transportation. The Indians used it as a portage, carrying their canoes from the Des Plaines River to the Chicago River, then paddling them to Lake Michigan. Possibly the first white men to use the Chicago portage were Louis Jolliet and Father Jacques Marquette, two French explorers. This was in 1673, on their way toward what is now Green Bay, Wisconsin. Marquette and two companions camped near the Chicago River in the winter of 1674–5.

The first permanent settler was the black man Jean Baptiste Point du Sable, who established a trading post on the north bank of the river in 1779. The Indians controlled the area until 1794, when General 'Mad Anthony' Wayne defeated them in the Battle of Fallen Timbers, and the Indians ceded to the United States 'One piece of land Six Miles Square at the mouth of the Chicakgo River.' There is an argument about what 'Chicakgo' or, more correctly, 'Checagou' means. No one doubts that it was an Indian word, but some historians say it meant 'skunk' or 'wild onion,' both of which are still fairly common in the area; others think it meant 'big,' 'great' or 'powerful.' It probably depends on how one feels about the city.

Soldiers under the command of Captain John Whistler (whose descendent, the painter James Abbott McNeill Whistler, was to memorialize his mother) built Fort Dearborn on the north bank of the Chicago River near what was then the lake front. This was in 1803, and by 1812 a small settlement had grown up nearby. But the Federal Government abandoned the outpost during the War of 1812, and the Indians massacred the settlers and burned the fort. It wasn't until 1816 that Fort Dearborn was rebuilt, and the settlement became a village two years later. Its boundaries weren't defined until 1830, when a commission mapped a proposed canal from

Opposite top: A 1928 photo of the property at 558 DeKoven Street where Mrs O'Leary's cow kicked over the lantern and started the Great Fire in 1871.

Opposite bottom: A 1930s photograph showing the Water Tower and the Palmolive Building with its Lindbergh Beacon.

Below: The Union Stockyards in the 1930s.

Ottawa (Illinois) to the west, to Chicago to the east, and laid out both towns. It wasn't until 1833 that Chicago was incorporated as a town. It became a city in 1837, with a population of only 4000 – but it was the seat of Cook County.

The city's real growth probably began in 1848, when the Illinois and Michigan Canal was completed, giving farmers to the west a chance to ship their products to the east by way of Lake Michigan. Between 1848 and 1850, Chicago's population rose from 20,000 to 30,000. Then, in 1856, the Galena and Chicago Union Railroad began operating, and Chicago's place as a transportation center was assured. By 1860, the year that Abraham Lincoln was nominated to run for president (the Republican Convention was held in Chicago), the city had 112,172 residents. By 1870 almost 300,000 people were living in the city.

Then came the great Chicago Fire in 1871, and the entire business district was wiped out. The fire raged for more than 24 hours, destroying 17,450 buildings and razing some 3⅓ square miles of the city. At least 300 people were killed, 90,000 were left homeless and $200 million worth of property was lost.

It was then that the motto of Chicago – 'I Will' – became a reality. The people of the city spat on their hands and rebuilt. So well did they do the job that a mere 19 years later there were more than one million people living in Chicago – making it the nation's second-largest city, second only to New York. In a way, the fire, tragic though it was, may have been a good thing for the city. Many of the slums were burned out, and the world's first skyscraper, the Home Insurance Building, was erected. Parks along Lake Michigan were planned. The downtown area came, over the years, from a dream to a reality. In 1893, just 22 years after the tragedy, Chicago held the World's Columbian Exposition on the South Side – a World's Fair celebrating the four-hundredth anniversary of the discovery of America by Christopher Columbus. Chicago had come back and was well on its way to becoming the Gem of the Prairie – a city of varied ethnic groups, artists, writers and architects.

People began to discover the city. Around the turn of the century Rudyard Kipling visited the area and wrote: 'I have struck a city – a real city – and they call it Chicago.' Carl Sandburg, the poet, had this to say in 1916:

Hog butcher for the world,
Tool maker, stacker of wheat,
Player with railroads
    and the nation's freight handler;
Stormy, husky, brawling,
City of the big shoulders.

BIRD'S-EYE VIEW UNION STOCK YARDS TODAY

Some people also call Chicago 'the Windy City,' but no one knows who coined that phrase. A J Leibling, a New York writer, called it 'the Second City.' Songwriter Fred Fisher called it 'That Toddlin' Town' in his song of 1922. Boosters call it 'the City That Works.' Frank Sinatra sings of it as 'My Kind of Town.' More than three million people today call it 'Home.' And the 31 percent of the United States population that lives within 500 miles of this metropolis call it simply 'the City.' Since 1818, when it became a village, wherever one looks in Chicago, it lives up to its motto – 'I Will.'

It was Armistice Day – 11 November 1918 – and 3½ million Americans were in uniform, over two million of them in Europe. Probably 20 percent of them were from the Chicago area, and when news of the war's end reached the city, Chicagoans went wild.

In the Loop – the business core of Chicago, so called because it is ringed by the elevated railroad tracks – office workers were throwing tons of paper from the windows of the tall buildings, automobile horns were honking, drunks were fighting and yelling and women were embracing any man in uniform. Musicians formed impromptu bands and improvised parades wound through streets so crowded that automobiles could not get through the packed intersections.

Novelist James T Farrell described it best in his book *Young Lonigan*. William 'Studs' Lonigan, aged 15, was in the Loop that day:

He suddenly looked up through the noises and falling paper, and there was Old Glory on a flag pole, furled in the breeze, glinting in the November sunlight – Old Glory that had never kissed the dust in defeat, and he could see it floating, flying over the trenches, ruins, corpses of the fields of France, again Victorious! Old Glory! His Flag! Proudly he told himself: 'I'm an American.'

Right: The botanical conservatory in Lincoln Park in the 1920s.

Opposite top: A scene at the Union Stockyards when Chicago was truly the 'hog butcher for the world.'

Opposite far left: Chicago's own James T Farrell (1904–1979), the author of *The Studs Lonigan Trilogy.*

A few weeks later a detachment from Chicago's own Black Hawk Division came through the city on its way to Camp Grant to be demobilized. They arrived at the La Salle Street Station on the morning of 13 January 1919. They marched west to the Old Coliseum and then back to Michigan Avenue, into the Loop, just before noon that day.

At 11:30 AM they fell out at State Street and Jackson Boulevard and the city gave them an all-out 12-hour hospitality party. As they boarded the train to Camp Grant around midnight, Colonel Philip R Ward, their commanding officer, said: 'These men can't say much, as they are too deeply stirred for words. It's the greatest thing I've ever seen or heard of. Old Chicago is showing her heart, which is as big as the world.'

A month later another enthusiastic welcome was given to 1278 black soldiers of the 370th United States Infantry. It was enthusiastic, but a bit different from the one given to the white troops. The social part of the welcome was handled by black Chicagoans, who planned banquets, receptions and dances at various halls and churches on the South Side, where most of them lived. Mayor William Hale 'Big Bill' Thompson of Chicago, who probably did have some sympathy for the blacks of the city, and certainly felt a need for their votes, said: 'There may be other battles yet to fight for our country, and if there should be, it is safe to predict that the Negro citizen and soldier of the future, like his ancestors of the past and present generations, may be relied upon to stand steadfast in support of the principles of our great republic.'

The war was over, and life – it seemed – would go back to normal again.

Below: The façade of the old Coliseum.

MANNERS
AND MORES

Previous pages: An artist paints in Garfield Park as onlookers watch him work – 1929. The dome of the park's administration building is in the background.

Far right: Skirts were pretty high in 1929. Here, Betty Holmberg, a waitress at the Old Town Grill of the Hotel Sherman, is sized up by Edward Kavassy, the maître d'hôtel, who claimed that he picked his waitresses 'like Ziegfeld picks his chorus girls.'

Opposite top: North Michigan Avenue in 1922. Chicagoans were in love with their cars and occasionally drove them too fast, as the sign attests.

Opposite bottom: The crowd around the bear cage at the Lincoln Park Zoo – 1921.

Below: A couple of 1930s lovelies.

A new age of experimentation began to dawn in 1919. Some fundamentalist preacher in Chicago decried the shifting of the hemlines being worn by women of the city's avant garde – 'Not since the days of the Bourbons has the woman of fashion been visible so far above the ankle.' Hemlines had climbed to six inches above the ground, but more was in store as they continued to rise. As far as lecherous men of Chicago were concerned, however, the effect was spoiled when the women insisted on wearing spats, high-laced walking boots or high patent leather shoes with contrasting tops of buckskin – to protect their ankles, they claimed.

The women were far from completely liberated. They still thought that only prostitutes wore flesh-colored stockings. And they clung to their habit of wearing chemises and petticoats. The use of powder was on the rise, but still they shrank from wearing lipstick or rouge. Hats with veils were in, as were demure bathing suits – outer tunics of silk or cretonne over tight knitted suits worn with long black stockings.

The men of Chicago kept their hair short and the women kept theirs long. After all, it was well known that short-haired women and long-haired men were either radicals or Bolsheviks or both – and they probably espoused the doctrine of free love into the bargain.

suit against the *Chicago Tribune*. He didn't help his case much when he declared from the witness stand that Benedict Arnold had been a writer, or, when asked if there had ever been a revolution in this country, he answered, 'Yes, in 1812.'

Chicago men were reading about that young left-handed pitcher breaking in with the far-off Boston Red Sox – a man by the name of George Herman Ruth. 'Babe' hit but one home run in April, then hit two in May 1919. He ended up, however, with 29 at the end of the season, which was a new record. More important was that Ty Cobb of the nearby Detroit Tigers led the league in batting. Other sports news that year included the Jess Willard-Jack Dempsey fight being staged in Toledo by Tex Rickard on the Fourth of July. Editorials said that 19,650 people were so depraved that they sat in a broiling sun to watch Dempsey take the six-foot six-inch Willard's championship away by a knockout in the third round.

The Chicago sports fan might have noticed in his paper that the 17-year-old Bobby Jones was becoming prominent on the golf links, but golf was not the society sport that it was later to become. Indeed, grown men who spent their time knocking a little white ball around the ground were laughed at, especially if they wore the latest style in golfing garb. If they wore knickers, or 'plus fours,' people might say to them, 'Get some man's pants.' The same was true for tennis, which had yet to become a popular ritual, despite the exploits of a young Bill Tilden.

Prices in 1919 were zooming – including

Above: Bobby Jones stands beside the Walker Cup, which the American golf team had just won from the British team in Chicago 1928.

Opposite top: Tezio Toba (left), the captain of the Japanese Davis Cup Team, and Bill Tilden, the captain of the United States Team, pose at the Chicago Town and Tennis Club after the Americans had defeated the Japanese in the American Zone Davis Cup finals in 1928.

Far right: Equestrians enjoy the bridle path in Washington Park.

Most Chicagoans had never heard of a vitamin.

What were Chicagoans reading in their many newspapers? (Chicago had newspapers for every taste at the time, but by 1927 its number of morning papers was to drop from seven to two because of mergers, the development of wire services and the proliferation of national chains.) They were reading about the progress of a Navy Seaplane, the NC-4, that was on a flight across the Atlantic, landing in the Azores Islands in May of 1919. Weeks later, Alcock and Brown flew the Atlantic in a single hop.

The Peace Conference at Paris was continuing – that Peace Conference which was to be so disastrous for President Woodrow Wilson – but Chicagoans didn't care. Europe might as well have been on the moon, as far as they were concerned. They were more caught up in the stories that urged an oversubscription of the wartime Victory Loan – the posters read, 'Sure, we'll finish the job.'

More and more servicemen were coming home. And Henry Ford was waging a libel

food, rent, clothing and taxes. Five years before, milk had been nine cents per quart. In 1919 it was 15 cents per quart. In the same five years, sirloin steak was up from 27 cents to 42 cents per pound. Butter had risen from 32 to 61 cents per pound and eggs from 34 to 42 cents per dozen. There was also a shortage of houses and apartments because of the servicemen returning home.

Chicagoans drove Lexingtons, Maxwells, Briscoes, Templars and the ubiquitous Ford Model T. But changes were just around the corner, because Walter Chrysler had just been elected to the first vice-presidency of the General Motors Corporation, and soon they would be considering the Chevrolet and other General Motors products, eventually including the Chrysler, after Walter changed jobs.

Probably only a little over 10 percent of the cars driven in Chicago were closed in 1919. The open car was the most popular, not only because of the extra cost, but because it was equated with vast riches. Indeed, self-starters still cost the customer extra money. But 1919 was the year that launched a driving revolution. In the next 10 years, registered automobiles in the United States would climb from seven million to 23 million.

In 1919 Chicago was still nervous about the motor car. There was a speed limit of 15 miles per hour in residential areas, but that was top speed. The speed limit then fell to ten miles per hour in built-up zones and dropped to six miles per hour on curves. This also took into account the miserable quality of roads, both in Chicago and in the nation in general. Most

of the highways were dirt; a few were gravel. And it took a long time to remedy this. For example, in 1937, in Michigan, two large cities only some 40 miles apart – Grand Rapids and Battle Creek – were connected by a narrow gravel country road.

After the Armistice, the Stock Market had gone down when government contracts were cancelled and workers were laid off. But now the factories were starting on a climb back, and some of them were running full tilt. In Chicago, it was a great year for parades. With the city elders on reviewing stands and flags waving, the soldiers' bayonets glistening in the spring sunlight, the bands playing 'The Long, Long Trail,' Chicago honored its heroes. But the heroes only wanted the fuss to be over, so that they could dress in civilian clothes again and sleep late in the morning.

A few society dances in the Chicago of 1919 featured jazz bands, but most of them hired traditional orchestras. These were the bands that droned on such songs as 'I'm Always Chasing Rainbows,' 'Smiles,' 'Dardanella,' 'Hindustan,' 'Japanese Sandman,' 'I Love You Sunday' and 'I'll Say She Does.' As a sign of a not-too-far-off trend, perhaps a younger couple could be seen 'petting' in the corner of the ballroom.

At these dances only a few women smoked, but they undoubtedly did it either self-consciously or defiantly. Between 1919 and 1930 cigarette consumption among women would more than double.

Chicagoans were going to the movies to see Charlie Chaplin in *Shoulder Arms* or Douglas Fairbanks (Sr) in *The Knickerbocker Bucaroo* or Mary Pickford in *Daddy Long Legs* or

Pickford again in D W Griffith's *Broken Blossoms*. They were staying home to play auction bridge – contract bridge had not been invented. When they had time to read, they were picking up Vincent Blasco Ibanez' *The Four Horsemen of the Apocalypse*, Booth Tarkington's *The Magnificent Ambersons*, Joseph Conrad's *Arrow of Gold*, Brand Whitlocks' *Belgium* or H G Wells's *The Undying Fire*.

Actually, Chicago parents didn't know what was going on with their offspring – who were soon to become the 'Flaming Youth' of the 1920s – until F Scott Fitzgerald, who was barely out of Princeton, told them in his novel *This Side of Paradise*, published in April of 1920. Now the old folks knew that petting had become a favorite indoor sport.

Women all over the country were growing in their independence. They even got the vote in 1920. And they were also being freed of household chores. Homes were getting smaller and easier to clean. Household appliances were becoming more popular. By 1924 90 percent of American homes would have electric irons. To make things even easier for the housewife, canned food sales were growing and commercial bakeries, delicatessens and laundries were proliferating.

These phenomena were beginning to free, not only the women of Chicago, but women all over the country, from their drudgery. They began to get jobs – not only in teaching, nursing, secretarial and stenographic, social service and clerical work. They were now getting into publishing, advertising, antiquing, running tearooms and working in department stores. Small-town girls were

Right: In the 1930s Jackson Park was a maze of lawn tennis courts.

Left: An interior shot of the Garfield Park conservatory, with its lovely Easter blooms, during a flower show in 1930.

Right: Mothers sunning their children in the idyllic setting of Lincoln Park – 1933.

Opposite top: Mah Jong, played with 12 dozen 'tiles' similar to dominoes, was one of the crazes of the 1920s in Chicago.

Opposite bottom: An outdoor painting class at Chicago's Art Institute – 1919 – strives to capture its exotic model on canvas.

borrowing money from their fathers so they could seek their fortunes in Chicago by getting employment at Marshall Field's and Carson, Pirie, Scott and Company.

No one knows exactly why – perhaps it was partly this departure by women from their traditional roles – but the divorce rate was on the increase. In 1910 only 8.8 out of one hundred marriages ended in divorce. In 1920 the figure had climbed to 13.4 per hundred marriages and would zoom to 16.5 in 1928.

As far as women's fashions were concerned, things were happening. In July of 1920 a fashion writer commented: 'The American woman ... has lifted her skirt far beyond any modest limitation.' These skirts were now nine inches above the ground. Modern young women, soon to be called 'flappers,' wore thin dresses that were either short-sleeved or sleeveless. And the more daring of them rolled their stockings below their knees, giving the shocked observer an occasional glimpse of kneecap.

Then, on 21 September 1920, Atlantic City has its first Miss America Contest. This widely publicized beauty pageant featured girls wearing one-piece bathing suits, and the dam had burst. No longer would young women be ashamed of their bodies. Less was more.

Many of these demure young things were now wearing cosmetics. Die-hard critics were heard to say 'The intoxication of rouge is an insidious vintage known to more girls than mere man can believe.' And some shocking girls were not wearing corsets anymore. One of them pointed out, 'The men won't dance with you if you wear a corset.'

In 1921 Chicagoans were reading another revolutionary book – Sinclair Lewis's *Main Street* – which planted the seed that the old-time morality of the small Midwestern town might not have been as ideal as they had long thought. On the other hand, they were also numbing their minds with Frederick O'Brien's page-turner called *White Shadows of the South Seas.*

Then, in 1922, came the craze that was to turn them all into Lotus-Eaters for the next few years – Mah Jong. This harmless yet habit-forming Oriental game, with its tiles and winds, became all the rage. Imports of the boards and equipment totaled $50,000 that year, and some of the more elaborate and upscale sets sold for $500 – not too far from the price of a Model T Ford.

In 1922 Chicago was still interested in popular music. All Chicagoans were singing 'Yes, We Have No Bananas,' a tune that stole its melody from Handel's 'Hallelujah Chorus' (*Messiah*), and the old Scottish folk song, 'Bring Back My Bonnie to Me.' They had also resurrected 'I Dreamt That I Dwelt in Marble Halls,' from the 1843 musical comedy *The Bohemian Girl*, by Michael William Balfe – an English composer who had been called, oddly enough, 'the British Bellini,' as if that were a term of approbation. Then there was the old favorite 'Aunt Dinah's Quilting Party.'

Nineteen twenty-four could fairly be called the year that the Roaring Twenties' Flaming Youth began their real revolution. And it might have been caused entirely by Henry Ford and his colleagues. Closed cars were in. From a figure of about ten percent in 1919, the percentage of closed cars had risen to 43 percent in just four years. By 1927 the percentage had risen to almost 83. This meant

Right: Richard Loeb (left) and Nathan Leopold Jr (center) in prison for the murder of Robert Franks in Chicago – 1924. Chicago lawyer Clarence Darrow defended them, and it was his novel exploitation of psychiatric evidence that averted a death sentence.

Below: Clarence Darrow in 1927 – two years after he had defended John Scopes, the Tennessee teacher who taught Darwin's theory of evolution, in the famous 'Monkey Trial' in Dayton, Tennessee. Darrow had a shambling figure, a drawl and an acid wit, and he was a major force in forming the conscience of his time by debating before the public a number of vital questions: racism, socialism, atheism, Prohibition, capital punishment and child labor.

that young people could get away from their parents, duennas and chaperones without freezing to death in an open car. The closed car was a movable room protected from the elements, and the youth of Chicago, always more motor-mad than any others, with the possible exception of Detroit youngsters, capitalized on this new form of transportation. One Chicago judge termed the closed car 'a house of prostitution on wheels.'

It was also during the mid-1920s that Chicagoans – both the kids and their parents – discovered sex magazines, confession magazines and the lurid motion pictures that were to be found if they kept their eyes open. As far as articles in magazines were concerned, one of them ran stories in the same issue entitled 'What I Told My Daughter the Night Before Her Marriage,' 'Indolent Kisses' and 'Watch Your Step-Ins.' The publishers had finally learned the gentle art of arousing the reader without arousing the censor. Confession magazines concentrated on mis-steps, describing vividly but always ending with a moral. A typical story was titled, 'The Confessions of a Chorus Girl,' but none of the articles were written by true confessors – rather by hack writers. An example of the genre was *True Story*, which had begun publication in 1919. Originally, it had about 300,000 subscribers, but by 1923 the circulation had climbed to 848,000. By 1925 it was at 1½ million and it hit 2½ million in 1926.

Chicagoans were also reading movie magazines in the mid-1920s. Many of them featured such lead-ins as 'Do you recognize your friend, Mae Busch? She's had lots of kisses but never seems to grow *blasé*. At least you'll agree that she's giving a good imitation of a person enjoying one [indicating picture].'

As far as movies were concerned, one picture advertised 'Brilliant men, beautiful jazz babies, champagne baths, midnight revels, petting parties in the purple dawn, all ending in one terrific smashing climax that makes you gasp.' Another announced 'Neckers, petters, white kisses, red kisses, leisure-mad daughters, sensation-craving mothers ... the truth – bold, naked, sensational.' Because of the lurid movies, the sensational press copy, and a few Hollywood scandals, Will Hays, who had been Warren G Harding's Postmaster-General, was brought in to police the movie industry, and his prudish rules lasted for a good many years. When he took over the job as official censor, he promised that 'This industry must have toward that sacred thing, the mind of a child, toward that clean virgin thing, that unmarked state, the same responsibility, the same care about the impressions made upon it, that the best clergyman or the most inspired teacher of youth would have.'

(He would later rule that 'virgin' was an unfit word to be heard in a motion picture.) In all this hullabaloo, Chicago's favorite song in 1924 was 'Barney Google (With His Goo-Goo Googly Eyes),' a song based on a popular comic strip.

Chicago's shift to the suburbs actually began during the mid-1920s. Developers built Colonial farmhouses with attached garages – how appropriate. They built Tudor cottages with sagging roofs that were made to look age-old – how authentic. They built Spanish stucco haciendas – adobe was not readily available in the Chicago area. In 1926 there were enough subdivisions staked out to accommodate the growth of the city for the next ten years, if the population kept increasing at the rate that it had been.

In the mid-1920s Chicago began to have second thoughts about its supercilious attitudes toward Midwestern values. One writer said: 'The civilized minority [in Chicago] were the ones who were members of the college-educated business class who could digest more complicated literature than that to be found in *The Saturday Evening Post* and *McCall's Magazine*. They read Sir Philip Gibbs' *Now It Can Be Told*, [John] Dos Passos' *Three Soldiers*, E E Cummings' *The*

Below: Clarence Darrow (seated on desk) at the Scopes trial in 1925. Scopes (in shirtsleeves) is seated behind him, arms interlocked, staring straight ahead.

Left: Some of the many bungalows that were built in Chicago during the building boom of the 1920s. Houses like these, often showing a Spanish influence, were going for from $7000 to $10,000.

Enormous Room. They were the ones who had sex because they learned its importance from Freud while others were having it because they liked it. [Sinclair Lewis's] *Main Street* in 1921 and *Babbit* in 1922 ... exposed the ugliness of the American small town, the cultural poverty of its life, without telling of its friendliness and generosity.'

From the 1920s into the 1940s, when people – movie stars, symphony orchestra conductors and personalities of every shape and size – went from New York to Los Angeles by train (which was the only way to travel) Chicago was the stopover. Each morning the *Twentieth Century Limited* from New York would deliver its passengers in a car that was switched from the New York Central to the Santa Fe Railroad; that afternoon the car would head toward Los Angeles. And every afternoon, the 'New York Car' would arrive from the west to be attached to the *Twentieth Century* for the run to New York. So 'anybody who was anybody' thought of Chicago as a great place to be seen, to stretch one's legs and to have a good meal.

In 1927 women's skirts climbed to knee-length, a height that would last until the Stock Market Crash in 1929. Also, women wanted boyishly slender figures. That meant that sales of corsets took another nosedive, and the market in brassieres was shaky. Silk or rayon stockings and underwear replaced cotton, and flesh-colored stockings were in, much to the disgust of the older generation. Short hair was popular: all the young women were wearing pageboy bobs.

This new hairstyle had its impact, not only on parents and grandparents, but also on hairdressers. Young women developed the habit of going to men's barbers for their new hairdos, figuring that male barbers would do a good job in cutting women's hair to look like men's. Fights started between the hairdressers in the beauty shops and the barbers in their traditionally male preserve; hairdressers wanted to stop the barbers from cutting women's hair. As one hairdressers'

magazine put it: 'The effort to bring women to barbershops for haircutting is against the best interests of the public, the free and easy atmosphere often prevailing in barber shops being unsuitable to the high standard of American womanhood.' Some barbers retaliated by asking for laws forbidding hairdressers from cutting hair unless they were also licensed barbers. Meanwhile, the small cloche hat was adopted as ideal for wearing over the bobbed or shingled hair, no matter who styled it.

Hairdressers may have complained, but beauty shops were flourishing because women were using more cosmetics and having facials, applying pomades and astringents, and having their eyebrows plucked. By

Opposite top: A 1925 traffic jam on Michigan Avenue near the main branch of the Chicago Public Library (left). This was in the days when double-decker buses were still seen on Michigan Avenue.

Below: The *Twentieth Century Limited* leaving for New York from Chicago's La Salle Street Station in 1929.

the end of the 1920s, the average use of cosmetics by the average adult American woman was astounding – over a pound per year of face powder, and eight rouge compacts. By that time there were 2500 brands of perfume on the market and 1500 brands of face creams.

In 1928 came a sort of forecast of the Depression when all Chicago was singing 'I Can't Give You Anything but Love, Baby.'

Nineteen twenty-nine, before the Stock Market Crash, was a banner year for Chicago. Its population had hit 3½ million people. Its construction from 1925 through 1928 had culminated in $1,390,000,000 worth of tangible property. The Michigan Avenue Bridge had been completed, opening North Michigan Avenue to the stores, boutiques and shops that would eventually become 'The Magnificent Mile,' stretching to the Drake Hotel.

Chicagoans were singing some new songs in 1929, such as 'Singin' in the Rain,' 'The Pagan Love Song' and 'I'm Just a Vagabond Lover.' But, of course, after the Wall Street Crash, they shifted to 'Happy Days Are Here Again.' They went to the movies to see Al Jolson in *Say It With Songs*, Joan Crawford in *Our Modern Maidens*, Ronald Colman in

Above left: The famous Pump Room of the Ambassador East Hotel.

Above right: All kinds of athletic events were held at Soldier Field after its completion – including this sparsely attended rodeo in 1926.

Left: One of the features of the elegant Pump Room at the Ambassador East was a flaming dinner served by a liveried waiter.

Bulldog Drummond ('*Mr* Colman's first all-talking picture') and Lew Ayres in *All Quiet on the Western Front*. After the crash, women's skirt lengths fell. Ruffles, frills and flounces were coming in and bobbed hair was going out. The red-hot baby had gone out of style.

The American people seemed to lose their former preoccupation with sex. Robert Benchley, who was a theater reviewer at the time, summed it up from his vantage point. 'I am now definitely ready to announce that Sex, as a theatrical property, is as tiresome as the Old Mortgage, and that I don't want to hear it mentioned ever again. . . . I am sick of rebellious youth and I am sick of Victorian parents and I don't care if all the little girls in all sections of the United States get ruined or want to get ruined or keep from getting ruined. All I ask is: don't write plays about it and ask me to sit through them.'

By 1931 Chicagoans were singing 'Life Is Just a Bowl of Cherries.' This song seemed to sum up the disillusionment and bewilderment of the Depression and try to take it lightly.

Chicago had one thing to cheer about in 1931, however. That was the year that Jane Addams of Hull House received the Nobel Peace Prize. Jane Addams (1860–1935) and a friend, Ellen Starr, had rented a house on the corner of Polk and Halsted Streets, furnished it with good family pieces and European art, and, on a cool autumn evening in 1889, opened the front door and let the neighborhood in. Hull House became a pioneer in American settlement work. Its volunteers established a day nursery and the city's first public playground, taught sewing and cooking and held Saturday night dances.

The starving were fed, the unemployed were given work and the neglected and beaten were given sanctuary. 'Jane's idea,' Ellen Starr wrote that first year, 'is that [settlement work] is more for the benefit of the people who do it than for the other class . . . that one gets as much as she gives.' At first Jane Addams paid all the expenses out of her own pocket.

Addams was born in Cedarville, Illinois, on 6 September 1860, the eighth of nine children. Her father was well off and sent her to medical school, but surgery for a congenital spine defect weakened her health and forced her to drop classes. Her doctor sent her abroad. In England she saw the poor eating off the street. In Germany she saw brewery

workers carrying on their backs huge wooden tanks filled with hot liquid that spilled over the sides, scalding their bodies. She lived four years in Baltimore, where she was relatively inactive and suffered from nervous depression, and then returned to Europe in 1887.

In London's East End she visited Toynbee Hall, a settlement started by a group of Oxford men who, influenced by British social critic John Ruskin and Leo Tolstoy, were trying to ease the suffering brought on by rapid industrialization. She decided to start a similar settlement in a crowded immigrant section of Chicago.

Her energy, diplomacy, warmth and bravery made Hull House a leader in broad areas of social reform. Under Hull House pressure, the State of Illinois passed its first factory inspection act, established the nation's first juvenile court, formulated child labor laws, streamlined welfare procedures and initiated compulsory school attendance. When garbage collection deteriorated, Addams got herself appointed garbage inspector and followed collectors on their rounds each morning, starting at 6:00 AM. When she forced the city to scrape years of accumulated dirt from the streets, the death rate in her district dropped from third to seventh in the city.

In the early 1900s, Addams also became involved in women's rights, politics and pacifism. 'It is easy to kill a man. It is not easy to bring him forward in the paths of civiliza-

Above: In the spring of 1930, this young man's fancy turned to thoughts of love – Lincoln Park.

Right: Nobel Prize-winner Jane Addams (left), the founder of Hull House in Chicago, discusses a charity concert with Ernestine Schumann-Heink, the former opera star, in April 1935.

tion,' she said, and shocked many of her backers by opposing America's entry into World War I. Because of her enthusiasm for the labor movement, many of Chicago's wealthy citizens came to fear her as a dangerous radical. But the common folk – those she had helped, and they numbered in the thousands – were her staunchest supporters. One of them said of her: '[Jane Addams], like the sunlight, shone alike on the just and unjust.'

She wrote hundreds of articles and books, and she lectured around the country. Although she had a weak heart, she kept up her pace, and in 1931 was co-recipient of the Nobel Peace Prize, sharing it with educator Nicholas Murray Butler. Chicagoans were to win many more Nobel Prizes – in literature, the sciences and particularly in economics – but Addams's prize was undoubtedly the most important. She never gave up the fight, because the conditions always remained. She once said of her neighborhood, 'The older and richer inhabitants ... move away. They make room for the newly arrived immigrants, who are densely ignorant of civic duties. Meanwhile, the wretched conditions persist.'

Nineteen thirty-one was also a year of

Above: Jane Addams (far right on sofa) holds a press conference on her role as an American peace advocate four years before World War II broke out in Europe.

Left: A 1902 photograph of Jane Addams, one of the most widely respected women of her time.

crazes in Chicago. Those who were not spending hours playing backgammon were learning the newfangled game called contract bridge, or playing the recently introduced slot machines. They lined up at movie theaters to see Jean Harlow in *Hell's Angels*, or Harry Carey in *Trader Horn*, or the new film star Edward G Robinson in *Smart Money*, or Gloria Swanson in *Indiscreet*.

And what were they reading? The big best-seller in town was Pearl S Buck's *The Good Earth*. But they also wanted a good laugh. The Depression and its miseries had made them turn from sex to laughter in their reading material, and the new magazine called *Ballyhoo* was just the thing. *Ballyhoo* ridiculed everything from business to politics to advertising, and its circulation quickly rocketed to more than one million readers.

Chicagoans who were able to afford cars went in for gimmicks, and the latest fashion was to have a car with free wheeling. The driver of an automobile with this option could pull a button on the dashboard and the car would coast when he took his foot off the accelerator. When he stepped on the gas again, the free wheeling went out and the engine revved up once more.

But the strangest fad of that year of 1931 was tree sitting. It seemed as if everyone were

out to set a new record for the length of time he or she could perch on a tree branch.

Pinball games were introduced in 1932, and it soon seemed as if every drug store, tobacco store, hotel corridor and restaurant in town boasted at least one. Other popular Chicago crazes of 1932 were punchboards, jar games, race track betting and bingo at the local church. People didn't have too much money to spend at movie theaters, so the exhibitors were forced to go in for some gimmicks. Bank night and dish night were started in 1932, and some theaters went in for bingo. But the big thing was the introduction of the double feature, in which the patrons got two pictures for the price of one.

It seemed that it was the kids who profited most from the theaters' efforts to bring in customers, especially on Saturday afternoons. Sometimes they could spend four hours being entertained for a modest ten cents, and there were some theaters that lowered their kids' admission price to five cents. It can be documented that on at least one Saturday afternoon at the Buckingham Theater, a young patron could see three feature films, five cartoons, the last chapter of

Above: A parade up State Street in celebration of the thoroughfare's newly inaugurated lighting system – 14 October 1926. President Calvin Coolidge, in Washington, had just pressed a button that turned on the power. Harold 'Red' Grange, the football star, was appearing in a vaudeville act at the Rialto Theater, which was later to become Chicago's premier burlesque house.

Left: A couple of intrepid Charleston lovers warm up on the roof of the Sherman Hotel.

Opposite: Chicago was building in 1929. Here a new skyscraper is going up, backed by (from left) – the Medinah Athletic Club, Tribune Tower and McGraw-Hill Building.

Following pages: The heart of 1930s Chicago, intersected by the Chicago River, as seen from Tribune Tower. Michigan Avenue is in the foreground, the Wrigley Building to the right.

Above: Looking north from the Chicago River along Michigan Avenue – 1929. In the distance to the right is the Allerton Hotel, whose Tip Top Tap on the top floor gave patrons the best aerial view in town.

Right: The Fort Dearborn Memorial at the Michigan Avenue Bridge over the Chicago River commemorates the site of the founding of Chicago. The relief shows the massacre of women and children by the Indians when the fort was surrendered. The memorial was erected in 1928.

Opposite: The dotted lines show the course that engineers laid out to straighten the Chicago River in 1926.

a serial and the first chapter of another serial. In addition, while they lasted, every kid was given a cardboard cowboy hat, a sack of clay marbles (which crumbled to dust on impact) and a packet of worthless foreign stamps (Switzerland and Weimar Republic Germany were the most prominent).

One favorable impact of the Depression on Chicago mores was that the divorce rate went down in 1932. Where it had been 1.66 per thousand marriages in 1929, it fell to 1.28 per thousand marriages in 1932. Of course, the reason was that divorces cost money.

Chicago was still movie-crazy when 1933 rolled around. Mae West was packing in the crowds in *I'm No Angel*, as was Katharine Hepburn in *Little Women*. And that was the year in which Walt Disney stunned the world with his animated all-color short *The Three Little Pigs*, and all Chicago was singing 'Who's Afraid of the Big Bad Wolf?' Other favorites that year were Ginger Rogers and Fred Astaire in *The Gay Divorce* and Gary Cooper in *Mr Deeds Goes to Town*, which introduced the word 'pixilated.'

Everyone was telling 'Knock-Knock' jokes in 1933, and it seemed as if everyone were

reading Hervey Allen's novel *Anthony Adverse*, a huge sprawling book that, pound for pound, gave the reader as much for his or her money as *Gone With the Wind* would later. Chicagoans warned one another not to drop the book on their foot.

Nineteen thirty-three was also the year in which Chicago was caught up in the latest game craze – Monopoly. When they were not trying to stay out of jail on the Monopoly board, Chicagoans were singing 'The Music Goes Round and Round.'

By 1935 even people in isolationist Chicago were beginning to notice how powerful Hitler and Mussolini were becoming in Europe. The big book that year was Sinclair Lewis's *It Can't Happen Here* – a novel about Fascism coming to the United States.

In 1936 the biggest phenomenon was the boom in sales of house trailers. The Depression was easing, and more and more people were deciding to take vacations, as long as they didn't cost a lot of money for hotel or tourist-cabin expenses. This was also the year when the whole country was reading Margaret Mitchell's *Gone With the Wind* and speculating about who would star in the film adaptation. Everyone knew that Clark Gable was made for the part of Rhett Butler, but who would play Scarlett O'Hara? Obviously, Bette Davis was the choice. How wrong can we be?

One of the strangest dances, 'The Big Apple,' came into being in 1937. Its silliness was not to be topped until 'The Lambeth Walk' arrived during World War II.

The big book of 1937 was a non-fiction effort by Dale Carnegie – *How to Win Friends*

Above: Two exhausted members of a walkathon team are ready to pass out at Leo Seltzer's Walkathon at the White City Casino on the South Side.

Right: Clarendon Beach where thousands braved the chill waters of Lake Michigan (1920s).

Opposite top: Marathon dancers at the Chicago Coliseum relax on cots during a break – June 1928

Opposite bottom: A marathon dance team in 1928. If they won, they would earn $3500.

Right: The most frightening roller coaster at Riverview Park was 'The Bobs'.

Opposite: A 1924 aerial view of Chicago's other amusement park – White City.

Below: The 119th anniversary of the Fort Dearborn Massacre was marked with ceremonies at the site of the fort at Wacker Drive and Michigan Avenue on 15 August 1931. The structure is the London Guaranty and Accident Building, which was where the fort stood. Buglers sounded taps at 9:00 AM, the hour at which the garrison and 40 settlers evacuated the fort. Ceremonies were also held at the actual site of the subsequent massacre, 18th Street and Prairie Avenue.

and Influence People – and all over Chicago people were being careful to call each other by name, as a form of flattery, as Carnegie had told them on page 1.

Another book came out in 1937 that was to become a minor classic. It was *Young Lonigan* by Chicago's own James T Farrell – the first book in his *Studs Lonigan Trilogy*, in which Farrell showed the world how the environment and the Depression got the best of a lower middle class Irish-American Catholic boy from the South Side of Chicago.

In 1937 all Chicago was flocking to the theaters to see Walt Disney's *Snow White*, the first full-length animated feature film. The city was singing 'Hi-Ho, It's Off to Work We Go,' 'I'm Wishing' and 'Some Day My Prince Will Come.'

John Steinbeck's *The Grapes of Wrath* appeared in 1939, telling of the plight of the Okies, those homeless migratory workers, and their trip to California, the promised land. Although Chicago and the rest of the country was coming out of the Depression, this book was a grim reminder of how bad things had been for the last ten years.

By 1939 there was a clear sign that Americans thought the Depression was nearly over. Skirt lengths had risen again – almost to the knee.

BOOM AND BUST

Although the United States had a slight recession in 1921, affecting chiefly the farmers, the general scene was one of prosperity. This was not caused, as some foreign critics supposed, by war profiteering, for World War I was actually an economic burden, increasing taxes and public debts and dislocating normal commerce. The chief cause of the mini-recession was the rapid spread of mechanization in industry. America was in good shape, and its citizens continued to buy their automobiles and appliances.

Indeed, in the decade of the 1920s, the Stock Market continued to rise, people had more disposable income than ever before, and many of them were getting rich.

One of the outstanding examples of the entrepreneur who became astronomically wealthy was Chicago's Samuel Insull. It was not possible to like the British-born Insull, who had been an official in the Chicago Edison Company and had made a fortune selling stock in what he called his holding companies. By 1929 he had control of three electric railways and hundreds of utility companies that sold electricity, gas, water, ice

and heat to more than four thousand towns on the Eastern Seaboard, in the Middle Atlantic States, in the South, the West, the Midwest and the Canadian Province of Ontario.

By the end of 1929, all this was lost, but Insull held on by borrowing some $90 million from banks. By 1932 it was found that his bookkeeping had been quite creative. For example, he had been listing expenses as assets. Also, while his investors were losing their money from 1929 to 1931, Insull had paid himself a salary of $1.4 million. It took until 1932 for the final collapse of Insull Utilities Investments. Insull himself declared bankruptcy and left the country. But he was brought back to the United States to face trial on the charges of fraud in bankruptcy, mail fraud and embezzlement. He was acquitted, but he remained a pariah. He returned to Europe, settled in Paris and died there in 1938.

However, a boom period can be followed by a depression, and people have understood this for generations. The United States had had major depressions in 1837, 1857, 1873

Previous pages: A Chicago free soup kitchen had many patrons during the Great Depression.

Below: A crowd outside a labor agency near the corner of Canal and Madison.

and 1893, as well as minor recessions. Each was acute for about three years and each had been preceded by a wave of speculations on stock markets.

The Great Depression that hit the United States was more severe and extensive than any of these, mainly because the nation had become more completely industrialized. Farmers are affected by the state of the market, but there is always some demand for food and, at worst, the farmers can raise their own. But when thousands of people decide that they cannot buy a new car, a factory closes down and hundreds of unemployed are turned out into the street. This, in turn, reduces effective demand and slows industry down even more.

One of the main causes of the Depression was of European origin. Recovery from World War I had been slow and only partial. Europeans could neither buy American goods nor pay back war loans to the United States Government. In several foreign countries, the currency had been inflated beyond recovery. The consequent dislocation of international trade was bound to affect the United States adversely. Another key factor was overproduction of consumer goods for which the market had dried up in the United States.

Then came 29 October 1929 – Black Tuesday – and the New York Stock Market crashed. In three days an estimated 15 billion dollars in market values had been wiped out in frantic selling, and, by the end of the year, some 40 billion. The mail-order and depart-ment-store firm of Montgomery Ward, whose stocks had been viewed as the harbinger of the new rising economic era, dropped from 83 to 50 in a mere two hours. Three million people were thrown out of work – a figure that would rise to an estimated 15 million in just two years.

Attempts were made, of course, to hold off the panic. Leading politicians and financiers made reassuring statements. They agreed that the nation was fundamentally sound, that the ruin of a few speculators was not the ruin of the country, and that 'prosperity was just around the corner.' But it took a long time to turn that corner. Reverberations from Europe aggravated the American situation. National income dwindled from 81 billion dollars in 1929 to 41 billion in 1932.

Americans knew that they were in trouble. One of the most popular cartoons showed a line of people waiting to get into a theater that was showing Charlie Chaplin in *City Lights*. The caption read, 'What's that? A bread line or a bank?'

Chicago, because of its hundreds of factories, its activities in transportation and its reliance on the products of the farms, was one of the cities hardest hit by the Great Depression. In the fall of 1930, the International Apple Shippers Association was faced with an oversupply of apples and had the brainstorm to sell them on credit to unemployed men at wholesale prices for resale at five cents apiece. Suddenly there seemed to be apple salesmen shivering on every street corner in Chicago.

'Hoovervilles,' little groups of tarpaper

Above: The deposed utilities magnate Samuel Insull (right) appears with his wife and their son, who was also charged with fraud, in a Federal Courtroom during their trial.

Above left: Samuel Insull entering the Cook County Jail.

Above: The Chicago Board of Trade opens its new securities market facilities on 17 September 1929, just over a month before the great crash.

Right: In 1930 selling apples was the only occupation for many of the unemployed in Chicago.

shacks that housed homeless families, seemed to blossom on every vacant lot in Chicago. At one of these Hoovervilles next to the garbage dump at 31st Street and Cicero Avenue, 300 people had established fair rules for taking turns at the garbage when a fresh dump came in. They had also developed certain tricks for using the garbage. They would scald bad meat and sprinkle it with soda, make soup from chicken feet and eat the pulp on melon rinds. They had also been able to furnish their makeshift shacks, made from packing cases, tarpaper and scrap iron, with junked automobile seats. Heat was provided outside by fires of rubbish in oil drums.

Unemployment in the United States in 1931 rose to an estimated 12 million jobless men, who went from office to office or factory gate to factory gate, only to hear, 'We'll let you know if anything shows up.' In Chicago, untenanted stores with 'To Lease' signs in the windows were everywhere. Few factory chimneys were smoking. There were fewer trucks on the street. There was no sound of riveters. Beggars and panhandlers

Left: In 1927 this Chicago stockbroker was busy with his latest toy – a private wire system direct to 40 of his customers.

ing, the company's founder, used his mother's maiden name for the firm, figuring that Curtiss was more American-sounding than Schnering (German surnames weren't too popular as the United States prepared to fight in World War I). The Baby Ruth bar first appeared in 1920, made of a chewy caramel center with peanuts, covered by chocolate. It immediately became a national hit as a five-cent bar. Over the years Schnering used ads featuring the 'Our Gang Comedies' troupe and the Dionne Quintuplets to push the Baby Ruth.

Below: A veteran selling apples on a Chicago street. Heavily industrialized Chicago was hit hard by the Depression.

were on the streets in unprecedented numbers. Trains were shorter and carried fewer Pullman cars. Fewer freight trains were on the line. Bread lines could be seen in the poorer neighborhoods. The homeless were sleeping on park benches or in doorways, and asking for left-over food at the back doors of restaurants. The number of hitchhikers was up – the result of a huge army of drifters looking for a place where there might be a job.

One writer, Louise V Armstrong, recorded a chilling scene in Chicago: 'One vivid, gruesome moment of these stark days we shall never forget. We saw a crowd of some fifty men fighting over a barrel of garbage which had been set outside the back door of a restaurant. American citizens fighting for scraps of food like animals.'

In 1932 Chicago had a local panic, indicating that it was worse off than most other cities. Nearly 40 banks went under in the city that year.

However, not everyone was suffering from the Depression. Construction of filling stations was booming, and only a few showed a drop in business during the Depression. People were still in love with their automobiles. And gas was cheap.

Another business that boomed during the Depression was the candy industry. People found that they could make a meal of a candy bar that cost just five cents. And Chicago was the center of this industry. Probably the first candy man to capitalize fully on the power of advertising was Otto Schnering. In 1923 he chartered an airplane and dropped Baby Ruth candy bars by parachute over the city of Pittsburgh, Pennsylvania.

The Curtiss Candy Company was founded in 1916 in a back room over a plumbing shop on Chicago's North Halsted Street. Schner-

Schnering not only believed in the efficacy of advertising; he also believed that it was his duty to provide employment for as many people as he could during the depths of the Depression. By this time he had four plants working night and day in Chicago – one of them making nothing but the penny-sized Baby Ruth. The plants were geared for four six-hour shifts, which gave more employment to more people than eight-hour shifts would have done.

Schnering also manufactured other candy bars. There were Butterfingers ('New delight, bite after bite after bite'), Baby Ruth Fruit Drops, Baby Ruth Mints, Peter Pan, Caramel Nougat, Coconut Grove and Buy Jiminy.

Schnering was also able to kill three birds with one stone with another Depression project in Chicago. He imported semi-professional hockey players from Canada and organized a hockey league – playing the games at the International Amphitheater at the Union Stock Yards. In one fell swoop, he provided more jobs (not only for the players but also for the workers at the games), entertainment (his employees and their fami-

Opposite top: United States marshals and Chicago police try to keep order during a run on a Chicago bank in the early years of the Depression.

Opposite bottom: Hundreds of the homeless and unemployed flocked to this Chicago soup kitchen.

Below: An indigent resident of a Chicago Hooverville cooks a meal. These down-and-outers called themselves 'The Lost Battalion.'

lies got free tickets) and advertising for his candy (the games between the 'Baby Ruths' and the 'Butterfingers' were particularly exciting). There was probably a tax deduction in there somewhere.

Another famous candy manufacturer was Mars Candies, which moved to Chicago in 1929 and came out with the Snickers Bar – still the most popular candy bar in America – in 1930. The company also manufactured the 3 Musketeers Bar, the Milky Way and the Mars Bar, among others.

Then there was the Reed Candy Company, with their Reed's Peppermint and Butterscotch confections; the Shutter-Johnson Company, with their Bit-O-Honey Bar; the Williamson Candy Company, with their Oh Henry! and Choc-O-Nuts; the Ferrara Pan Candy Company, with their Jaw Breakers, Atomic Fire Balls, Red Hots and Boston Baked Beans; and E J Brach & Sons, with their variety of chocolate flavored candy bars. And no one can forget that Wrigley's Gum and Cracker Jack were made in Chicago.

Another Chicago enterprise that prospered during the Depression was education. Not that the teachers themselves were prospering, but the quality of education given to Chicago children was certainly going up. Teachers were lucky to have jobs in those times, and the competition for the jobs was stiff: the Board of Education could get the pick of the college graduates to teach in the schools. The result was a fine education, and more people were getting it – attendance had never been higher, especially in the high schools, because

the students couldn't get jobs on the outside. There wasn't much extra money for education, and some students attended classes in one-room wooden 'annexes,' heated by pot-bellied stoves. These were often erected on the edges of school playgrounds, but the education inside was just as good as if the students were enrolled in a private school.

When people have suffered severe economic loss, they are apt to turn against any government then in power. The European Depression brought Hitler into power in Germany and deposed the king in Spain. The United States had always escaped revolution, but it is notable that each great depression has been followed at the next general election by political reversal. In 1840 the Democrats suffered their first defeat in four decades, when the Whigs elected William Henry 'Tippecanoe' Harrison. In 1860 the Republicans first came to power; in 1876 the Democrats were so close to winning that the result hung in doubt long after the election; in 1896 the Republicans displaced the Democrats.

The Depression made a Democratic victory in 1932 inevitable. It was not that President Herbert Hoover had not tried to do something about the Depression. He had instituted a Reconstruction Finance Corporation to bolster weak links in the national economy. But he was fundamentally a self-made individualist and did not wish to take the Federal Government too deeply into the sphere of direct charity. By 1932 the United States was ready for far more drastic remedies, and the people wanted a change.

Hoover was renominated, but neither he nor his party had much hope for victory. The Democratic Convention in Chicago was a short but bitter contest between Alfred E 'Al' Smith, the nominee four years earlier, and Franklin D Roosevelt, who was easily nominated. Roosevelt literally flew in the face of convention when he decided not to wait to be notified at home and hopped a plane to Chicago to give his acceptance speech at the Convention, telling those assembled, 'I pledge myself to a new deal for the American people.'

Roosevelt was as easily elected as he had been nominated. In 1928 Hoover had 21 million popular votes to Smith's 15 million and carried 40 states. In 1932 he had fewer than 16 million popular votes to Roosevelt's almost 23 million and carried only five states.

Before Roosevelt was inaugurated, however, he was involved in a tragedy. While he was riding in an open car in Miami with Mayor Anton 'Tony' Cermak of Chicago, he was attacked by a crazed assassin named Zangara, who fired a shot at Roosevelt and hit

Right: Franklin Delano Roosevelt (left), then governor of New York State, talks with Chicago's mayor Anton 'Tony' Cermak before the Depression thrust FDR into the presidency.

Opposite top: Franklin D Roosevelt making his acceptance speech after being nominated the Democratic Party's presidential candidate – Chicago, 1932.

Opposite bottom: The great army of the unemployed in Union Park – the only park in Chicago where 'soap-box' orations were allowed.

Below: The truck convoy used to transport the Chicago contingent on the 'National Hunger March' on Washington to protest the economic problems caused by the Depression. Participants left the trucks to march through the various cities en route to the capital.

Cermak, who died a few days later of his wounds. It has since been a bit of Chicago folklore that Cermak would have gone down in history as the speaker of the finest last words of all time if he had been more of a grammarian. Allegedly – and this is probably apocryphal – he said, 'I'm glad it was me instead of him.'

In his inaugural address, Roosevelt sounded a note of confidence. He pointed out that American resources were as great as ever and that the nation had 'nothing to fear but fear itself.' During his first 'hundred days' in office, he urged Congress to adopt an unpre-

cedented number of emergency measures. Collectively these were called the New Deal, from a phrase of Mark Twain's that Roosevelt had used in his acceptance speech, although it reminded some people of Franklin's cousin Theodore's Square Deal and Woodrow Wilson's New Freedom.

In proposing and implementing the New Deal, Roosevelt was assisted by his friend and advisor Harold Ickes. A Chicago lawyer, Ickes had formed his social philosophy at the University of Chicago and Hull House. He was appointed Secretary of the Interior by Roosevelt, and stayed on the job throughout

the Roosevelt presidency, from 1933 to 1945, with an additional year to assist Harry S Truman.

To provide jobs for the unemployed, Roosevelt suggested the Works Projects Administration (WPA), the Public Works Administration (PWA) and the Civilian Conservation Corps (CCC). Soon many Chicago families were affected by these projects. Parents said goodbye to their jobless sons, who were finally getting a chance to earn money planting trees and restoring the land with the CCC. Families were going to free concerts presented by WPA bands and orchestras. School children saw WPA workers building new facilities around their schools. And many public buildings sported new murals painted by WPA artists.

Roosevelt's National Recovery Act (NRA) had a broader aim: to organize a code of fair practice for each industry, shorten the work week, ban child labor and establish minimum wages. Soon Blue Eagle signs, with their slogan 'We Do Our Part,' were blossoming in store windows all over town and appearing in ads in all the papers.

The Agricultural Adjustment Administration (AAA) attempted to raise farm prices by restricting crops and slaughtering excess pigs. Both the NRA and the AAA, those two comprehensive measures, were declared

Above: The shooting of Chicago Mayor Anton J Cermak – 9 December 1933. The fatally wounded Cermak was assisted from the scene of the shooting in Bay Front Park, Miami, Florida, by local officials. Cermak lingered for several days before he died, the victim of assassin Giuseppi Zangara, who had meant to kill President Roosevelt.

Left: Harold Ickes, the Chicago lawyer who became Secretary of the Interior under Franklin D Roosevelt.

Opposite top: The men of the 'Hoover Hotel' line up on the lower level of Wacker Drive in 1930 for free food. 'Tokens' worth 20 cents were being sold to the public to give to panhandlers in the Loop, who could exchange them for a meal and a night in the Cook County Jail.

Opposite bottom: President F D Roosevelt (third from left), flanked by his wife, Eleanor and Chicago's new mayor, Edward Kelly, visit the gravesite of the murdered Mayor Cermak in 1933.

unconstitutional by the Supreme Court as exceeding the powers of Congress. But they had made their point. To raise prices, the gold content of the dollar was decreased and the United States (as had already happened in several European countries) was placed on a paper currency basis.

The only true experiment in government ownership was the Tennessee Valley Authority (TVA), which involved public generation of electricity in open competition with private power. Congress ended Prohibition and cancelled the national regulation of the liquor industry.

Obviously, changes so many and so great were bound to cause a reaction. Conservative former Democrats, including the national candidates in previous elections, John W Davis (1924) and Alfred E Smith (1928), seceded from the party. A 'Liberty League' was organized to oppose Roosevelt's liberalism (not the only time in American history

when contending factions have both appealed to 'liberty'). When Roosevelt tried to override the decisions of the Supreme Court by enlarging the court and thus giving the president a chance to appoint new men, Congress balked on the grounds that this might undermine the independence of the judicial branch of the government. It was the president's first major defeat, Later, however, deaths and resignations of some judges and the shift of opinion of others enabled Roosevelt to achieve his aims by other means.

Still, despite the new president, things were not exactly rosy in Chicago. By 1933 employment in the city's industries had been cut in half. Payrolls were down 75 percent. Property foreclosures went up from 3184 in 1929 to 15,200 in 1933. More than 163 banks had closed.

So many people had been dispossessed that the Chicago Urban League reported that 'Every available dry spot and every bench in the west side of Washington Park is covered by sleepers.' The unemployed scoured the streets and alleys for firewood and scraps of garbage, and thousands of jobless men slept under double-decked Wacker Drive and Michigan Avenue, which became known as the 'Hoover Hotel.'

Even the rich were affected. Colonel Robert Rutherford McCormick, publisher of the *Chicago Tribune*, had to sell some properties – *Liberty* magazine, for example. He also abolished the newspaper's bonus system and cut salaries, to make things even.

Teachers and some other city employees were paid in scrip currency in 1933. This meant they were holding the city's IOUs, and they had problems getting grocers to take the chits without claiming a discount. One of Franklin D Roosevelt's advisors, the Texas businessman, Jesse Jones, worked on this problem. He was able to get money from the Reconstruction Finance Corporation to pay the teachers and other civil servants, who were not only being paid in scrip but had taken a 26-percent pay cut. They got their cash in August 1934.

In the next election, Roosevelt had adversaries from the Left as well as from the Right – not only from the Socialist and Communist Parties, whose opposition might be expected, but from a strange catch-all Union Party led by Gerald L K Smith of the old Huey Long machine in Louisiana. It included Father Charles Coughlin, a priest who broadcast on the radio from Dearborn, Michigan, once a friend of Roosevelt's, now a bitter enemy. And Dr Francis Townsend, who had his own pet scheme for old-age pensions to replace Social Security, the money to be rapidly spent to stimulate commerce. In essence, it was a new Populism that they espoused.

In spite of these defections, Roosevelt was easily re-elected over Governor Alfred 'Alf' Landon of Kansas, the Republican nominee. In a sweep as unexpected to the victors as to the vanquished, Roosevelt carried 46 states, leaving only Maine and Vermont to Landon, who lost even his home state. The Depression was not quite over, but the recovery was sufficiently marked to give Roosevelt an unprecedented triumph.

The Democrats had achieved a new majority by putting together their three traditional elements (the Solid South, the party machines in the urban East and the rural radicals of the West) with the bulk of the poor, the foreign-born ethnics and the blacks, hitherto Republican, but grateful for new jobs.

But happy days were not completely here again. As Chicago poet Carl Sandburg said it:

Stocks are property, yes.
Bonds are property, yes.
Machines, land, buildings are property, yes.
A job is property,
No, nix, nah, nah.

Opposite: The American Legion parade passes down Michigan Avenue past the Art Institute (right). The Legionnaires had their national convention in the city in 1933.

Below: The beloved poet Carl Sandburg (1878-1967), who worked as a reporter for the *Chicago Daily News* for many years, in a photo by Edward Steichen.

JAZZ AND SWING

Jazz began somewhere in the vicinity of 1870 in the city of New Orleans. The instruments of its expression were the cornet, the clarinet, the trombone and the drums. The black street bands, the earliest development, had alto and baritone horns. The black dance bands, beginning in the 1890s, added piano, banjo and tuba. All kinds of music went into the mold – work songs, hymns, blues, marches, ballads, minstrel tunes and folk songs brought to America by Italian, Irish, Spanish and French immigrants. It all came out jazz. The players also originated basic melodies and performed them for their fellow musicians, who contributed their improvisations, different each time the tune was played. Later this technique was adapted to any popular song. The melody was just an idea, a base on which to build variations.

The bands played for parades, for picnics, for funerals, in honky-tonks, at carnivals and on riverboats. Often they climbed into wagons and drove through the streets to advertise the dances at which they were to play that night. The tailboard of the wagon was dropped, and there the trombone player sat, his feet dangling. Thus a trombone in a jazz band is still referred to as 'tailgate.' When

two rival bands met at a street corner, they locked wagon wheels and 'cut' each other, blasting away with their instruments until one or the other group, winded and temporarily deaf, gave up and pulled away. The remaining band was declared victorious by the crowd that assembled, and its dance that night was the better attended. The best of the bands was Buddy Bolden's. Bolden was a barber by profession; he also published a scandal sheet and was a heller with women. When his band marched down the street, he had a woman to carry his coat, a woman to carry his cap and a woman to carry his horn when he wasn't playing. He easily won both of his popular titles, 'Kid' and 'King.' He enjoyed his fame, worked hard to enhance it, and went mad during a parade in 1907.

There was a funeral almost every day. In New Orleans, where people must be buried above ground because of the marshy soil, interment was dramatic. Burial societies abounded among the blacks, and a man had to be a pauper not to go to his mausoleum with music. On the way to the cemetery the band played appropriately; one of the stock pieces was 'When the Saints Go Marching In.' When the ceremony was finished and the march back home began, the tempo quickened. The cornets sounded an introduction to 'Didn't He Ramble, He Rambled Round the Town Till the Butcher Cut Him Down.' After that, anything went, while the 'second line' of admiring urchins danced and accompanied the musicians with their own improvisations on homemade instruments. On Sundays there were baseball games in Washington Park and picnics at Milneberg on Lake Pontchartrain. In the repertory of every band was 'Milneberg Joys.' Among the famous bands were the Excelsior, the Eagle, the Diamond and the Reliance. After King Bolden, the best cornet players were Freddie Keppard, Joe Oliver and Louis Armstrong.

The cornet player was the boss because he played the lead. He blew it loud and he blew it strong. When Keppard played vaudeville with the Creole Band, no one could sit in the front rows of the orchestra. He blew them back to the middle of the house. The clarinet raced around the melody like a high-strung child, dashing in and out, climbing and falling on its face. The trombone, slurring, insinuating and marking the time, was sometimes a part of the rhythm section, sometimes a contestant in the melodic commentary. The drums and bass and banjo and, later, the piano, marked the beat. The method of slapping the bass fiddle had an obvious origin. A player broke his bow during a performance and had to resort to plucking the strings; the result was so effective that it became standard practice for jazz band players. The snare and

Previous pages: Benny Goodman (standing) played his clarinet with his orchestra many times in his old home town, Chicago. Here they are in 1939.

Below: The legendary pianist and composer 'Jelly Roll' Morton in a photograph taken in 1940.

bass drums of the marching band acquired appurtenances when they no longer had to be played and carried at the same time. Tom-toms, wood blocks and triangles grew on them like Spanish moss. The piano, a solo instrument by nature, began edging its way into solo parts as soon as it was adopted by the dance bands.

The piano began its career in jazz in 1897, the year New Orleans decided to confine prostitution within a certain area. Twelve blocks were marked out in the French Quarter, one of them being Basin Street. The ordinance creating the section was introduced by an alderman named Sidney Story; the most famous red-light district in the world was therefore called Storyville. It was fabulous from the beginning. It had its own 'blue book.' It had all kinds of prostitutes, some of them beautiful beyond belief. It had rows of 50-cent cribs and five-dollar houses with interiors resembling Hapsburg palaces. It had barrel houses where, for a nickel, customers filled their glasses from a cask and the spigot dripped whiskey into a gut bucket on the floor. There were gambling joints, cabarets, honky-tonks and approximately 200 places where, on a basic theme and with a sliding price scale, love was improvised. It was just the place for a vital, uninhibited, noisy, growing art form.

The bands played in the cabarets: they were too loud and distracting for the bordellos – the madams preferred string ensembles and piano players. One of these pianists was 'Jelly Roll' Morton, composer of 'Milneberg Joys.' It was Morton who adapted 'Tiger Rag' from a French quadrille. Another was Clarence Williams, who wrote 'I Ain't Gonna Give Nobody None of My Jelly Roll' and 'Pullman Porter Blues.' Still another was Tony Jackson, who had a song called 'I've Got Elgin Movements in My Hips with Twenty Years' Guarantee.'

At the cabarets, pianos were included in the bands. There, in the century's early years, were such men as Joe Oliver, Kid Ory, Jimmy Noone, Johnny and Baby Dodds, Freddie Keppard, Sidney Bechet and Louis Armstrong. The oldest profession sponsored the newest of the arts. Jazz grew and flowered in Storyville; its finest virtuosi were nourished there.

In Chicago at the end of World War I, very few people had heard of this new music. At their dances, the only modern thing that they heard was the moan of the saxophone, which had become the dominant instrument of the dance band, replacing the violin. The young men and women of Chicago were dancing the fox trot as if they were glued together. Nice girls smoked and drank a little, although some became 'blotto,' in the euphemism of the day.

Left: The great blues composer and singer Clarence Williams, who got his start in Storyville, New Orleans' fabled red-light district.

The boys carried hip flasks and there was a little petting and necking going on.

Not that one couldn't hear jazz in Chicago. But the city was not yet what Ben Hecht would call 'The Jazz Baby by the Lake' – the jazz capital of the universe. It was later that Chicago became 'That Toddlin' Town.'

All of this might not have happened if it hadn't been for the United States Navy. It was at the Navy's request that the New Orleans Police closed down Storyville in 1917: apparently, it was felt that the sailors were being corrupted in this area of prostitutes, hoodlums, gamblers and – jazz. The high-priced girls rode off in style. The residents of the cribs marched away with their

Below: Baby Dodds, the legendary drummer, who also came north from New Orleans.

mattresses on their backs. The musicians were in trouble. Most of them were black, and they faced the problem of intense segregation in New Orleans – they were not allowed to play outside Storyville. That left them employment only in the New Orleans funeral bands, and that just didn't pay the rent.

The only thing left for them was to play on the riverboats, some of which had been converted into excursion steamers. Many of these fine musicians joined the bands that entertained passengers aboard the boats that went up the Mississippi River and along its tributaries. They played their music at all the river towns. In the afternoon there would be excursions with dancing and picnic lunches, attended by mothers, nurses and children. In the evening young couples would go on moonlight cruises and dance to the music.

So jazz advanced northward, heading for Chicago and infecting Memphis and St Louis along the way. Far up in Iowa, at Davenport, a boy in short pants named Leon 'Bix' Beiderbecke heard the bands and decided that he would become a jazz musician. At Cape Girardeau a young pianist named Jess Stacy met each boat – later he played on one of them.

Chicago was ready for the refugees. Out on the South Side they had been listening to jazz since before the war – jazz that was heard all over the country on records played on countless Pathé, Brunswick and Victrola wind-up phonographs. They had been listening to Jelly Roll Morton, Tony Jackson, the Original Creole Band and another unusual combo – Tom Brown and His Dusters – unusual because the musicians in it were all white. Brown and his band played in the Lamb's Cafe on the corner of Clark and Randolph Streets for two weeks in 1914, and it was in that cafe that the word 'jazz' was coined. The restaurant was having trouble with the unions, and some of the striking employees tried to get back at the owner by insulting the music. Brown's band was 'nothing but jass,' they said, 'jass' being a colloquialism of the 22nd Street brothels, not in general usage outside of Chicago. The management made hay out of this, advertising the musicians as 'The "Jass" Band.' The idea of jass music suddenly became fascinating. The slander backfired, and the Lamb's Cafe was crowded every night. The next year, when another band came from New Orleans to Chicago, it was known as the 'Dixie Land Jass Band.' Later, the word jass got slightly cleaned up and became jazz.

Chicago restaurateur Mike Fritzel had also been featuring this kind of music at his Ansonia on West Madison Street for a long time. And when an all-white band called the New Orleans Rhythm Kings came to town, he booked them at his Friars' Inn on the corner of Wabash and Adams Streets.

Nineteen-eighteen was the year when the first surge of black jazzmen began to arrive in Chicago, bringing their ragtime and blues with them. Actually, it was all the blues – 'Jelly Roll Blues,' 'Wang Wang Blues,' 'Milneberg Joys,' 'Tailgate Blues,' Gut Bucket Blues,' 'Empty Bed Blues.' As Wingy Manone, the trumpeter, was to say, 'Man, isn't everything the blues?'

Chicago's South Side gave jazz a sincere welcome. When King Joe Oliver arrived in 1918, representatives of two bands met him at the La Salle Street Station. They knew that Oliver could play his cornet better, longer and louder than anyone. Eddie Venson wanted him to play at the Royal Gardens (later Lincoln Gardens) at 31st Street and Cottage Grove Avenue, with the Jimmy Noone Band. Bill Johnson, the leader of the band at the Dreamland at 35th and State Streets, brought along his great clarinetist, Sidney Bechet, to persuade Oliver to join them. The discussion shifted from the station to a bar and reached an amiable decision. Oliver ended up joining both bands. The Royal Gardens closed earlier than the Dreamland, and Oliver was to hop from the Royal Gardens to the Dreamland after the Gardens closed.

There was no one to challenge Oliver's title of 'King' except Freddie Keppard. Keppard dropped in at the Royal Gardens one night, and Oliver took him on in a 'cutting' contest. The consensus was that 'Joe Oliver beat the socks off Keppard.'

Back in New Orleans, where he was born in 1885, Oliver learned music slowly. He began in formal fashion, reading notes and playing with a children's band. Once, the children's band went on tour and Joe returned with a scar over one eye – someone had hit him with a broomstick, and for a while he was called 'Bad Eye' Joe. When he first played with the Eagle Band, he was sent home because he played 'so loud and so bad.' He was confused because the players improvised instead of following the score. Gradually, he learned the technique of improvisation and eventually produced a stomp of his own, called 'Dippermouth.'

Oliver went to work in Storyville, where he heard nothing but praise for Freddie Keppard and Manuel Perez. It irritated him, because he believed he was better than either one. He played in a cabaret at the corner of Bienville and Marais Streets, in a band with 'Big Eye' Louis on clarinet, Deedee Chandler on drums and Richard Jones at the piano. One night, between numbers, the musicians began talking about Keppard and Perez. Oliver stood up and walked to the piano. 'Jones,' he said,

Opposite: One of the most popular dance bands of the swing era was that of Tommy Dorsey (standing).

'beat it out in B flat.' Jones began and Oliver put his cornet to his lips and blew. He walked out into the street and pointed his horn first at the cabaret where Keppard worked, then at the cafe where Perez was playing. He blew with such power that every bed and bar in the neighborhood emptied. People poured into the street and crowded around Joe while he blew and blew, swinging his cornet from one target to the other. When everyone knew what he was doing, and was satisfied with the way he was doing it, he turned and led the people inside. After that he was 'King' Joe Oliver.

In Chicago, in 1920, Oliver organized his own Creole Jazz Band and took it to California. Returning to the South Side, he went to the Dreamland with his band, which featured a group of immortals – Johnny Dodds on clarinet, Honoré Dutray on trombone, Ed Garland on bass, Baby Dodds on drums and Lil Hardin (who later married Louis Armstrong) on piano.

Elsewhere in Chicago, Kid Ory could silence a room full of drunks by playing his trombone, and thirsty whites soon learned that they could hear superior jazz music and sip some not-so-superior booze by heading to the area between State Street and Calumet Avenue on 35th Street: to the Sunset Cafe, the Plantation, the Dreamland, the Panama, the DeLuxe, the Fiume, the Elite and the New Orleans Babe's. Besides these speakeasies, there were the theaters – the Vendome, the Big Grand and the Monogram – where jazz bands played. There were dance halls like Lincoln Gardens.

While all this was going on on the South Side, young music lovers on the North Side were going to dances at The Casino, where they could always slip out and head for Quigley's Speakeasy on Rush Street. Then it was off to the South Side to listen to 'Room Rent Blues,' 'High Society Rag' and 'Working Man Blues.' Out of all this came Chicago Jazz – a sort of New Orleans style with the Midwest thrown in – the concert in the courthouse square, with the musicians playing with precise control, yet hitting the high notes with assurance.

In 1922 King Oliver sent word to Louis Armstrong that he wanted him for his band for $30 per week. Armstrong had learned to play the cornet in the Waif's Home in New Orleans, to which he was sent for firing a pistol inside the city limits on New Year's Day 1913. Before that he had haunted Storyville at night, singing in an urchins' quartette, playing on a guitar made from a cigar box. As he grew, he played in cabarets, gin mills and

Below: Louis Armstrong, the immortal trumpeter and vocalist (center), sings as Jerry Colonna, the comedian (left), hams it up and bandleader Paul Whiteman listens appreciatively. It was in Chicago that Armstrong got his first big break.

barrel houses. He spent two seasons with Fate Marable's band on the Strekfus Line riverboats. He composed a tune which later became very popular and sold it for 50 dollars. He was 22 when he arrived in Chicago on the night of 8 July 1922. He stood outside the Lincoln Gardens and listened to the music, afraid to go in. He said later that he was thinking, 'I wonder if I'm good enough to play in that band.' He was. People used to say to Oliver, 'That boy will blow you out of business,' Oliver would smile and say, 'He won't hurt me while he's in my band.'

Before the white patrons began to pack the jazz joints on the South Side, there were white boys gathered around the bandstands at the Dreamland and the Lincoln Gardens, some of them barely out of kneepants. They were young musicians discovering the new music and listening to its masters. At home these boys practiced and listened to records by the New Orleans Rhythm Kings and the King Oliver Band. They were determined to play jazz. They formed small orchestras, played at school dances, and went to the South Side or the Friar's Inn to hear their idols. It was this group of kids that eventually created the real Chicago style of jazz.

Chicago style was, of course, based on a New Orleans style – the blues – but it was a departure from ragtime. Ragtime was smooth and relaxed – hot, but effortless. In Chicago style, the beat was pushed up and the music was frenzied and intense. New Orleans musicians looked like they were having a good time – always smiling. Chicago musicians concentrated, contorted their faces, and were exhausted after playing for half an hour. It was the Chicago style that was to endure.

The nucleus of the Chicago style jazzmen was a group of kids who attended Austin High School on the West Side. The Chicago Public Schools were always big on band music, and in the early 1920s all the high school bands participated in band contests at Riverview Amusement Park on the North Side, at Belmont and Western Avenues. In one year it would have been possible to see these high school bands with Bud Freeman playing sax for Austin, George Wettling playing drums for Calumet High School and Gene Krupa playing drums for Fenger High School.

Basically, the Austin High crowd included Frank Teschmaker (clarinet), Bud Freeman (C-melody and tenor saxophone), Jimmy McPartland (cornet), Dick McPartland (banjo and guitar) and Jim Lannigan (piano). Lannigan was the only one to desert jazz – he later played with the Chicago Symphony for 10 years.

Near the Austin High School building was a drug store and soda fountain called The

Spoon and Straw, and after school this group of gawking kids gathered there in their kneepants to wear out juke-box records like 'Tin Roof Blues' by the New Orleans Rhythm Kings. But at night they would head for the music on the South Side, and there they ran into some other young, white, aspiring jazzmen – many of them from Chicago, too.

Benny Goodman (clarinet) was attending

Above: Two of the all-time great jazz musicians, who also got their big break in Chicago – Peewee Russell (on clarinet, left) and Bud Freeman (on saxophone).

Below: Another Chicago boy, Gene Krupa, the master of the drums. At left is Buddy Wise on sax.

Lewis Institute (a prep school for those unable to get into the better schools and those who had been thrown out of them). Gene Krupa (drums) was an alderman's son hoping to study for the priesthood. Joe Marsala (clarinet) was a truck driver who liked to move pianos because he loved music. Dave Tough (drums) was from Oak Park and went to Lewis Institute with Benny Goodman. Art Hodes (piano) was already playing at the Rainbow Cafe on the West Side. Francis 'Muggsy' Spanier (cornet) was a tough Irish kid from the South Side.

Other Midwestern boys started showing up on the South Side, too. Three of them were Eddie Condon, William 'Red' McKenzie and Bix Biederbecke. Albert Edwin Condon was born 16 November 1905 in Benton County, Indiana, and came to Chicago from Momence, Illinois, by way of Chicago Heights. His basic instrument was the banjo, although he soon shifted to the guitar. He was small, quick-moving, clothes conscious, sharp-tongued, seldom still and forever organizing parties, dates, and excursions to the South Side. They called him 'Slick.' He was inno-

cently frank with phonies; otherwise he talked in a mixture of understatement and hyperbole. About Louis Armstrong's cornet playing he would say, 'It doesn't bother me.' In describing Gene Krupa to George Wettling, he said, 'He's got a 72-inch heart.' Condon was passionately, deeply devoted to jazz, proselytized constantly on its behalf, refused to solo on his own instrument, and pioneered in the appreciation of Beiderbecke.

Red McKenzie was an ex-jockey, born in Holy Name Parish in St Louis in 1899, the last of 10 children. After breaking both arms in his chosen profession, he retired and became a bellhop at the Claridge Hotel in St Louis. Standing on the sidewalk waiting for patrons to arrive, he would amuse himself by folding a piece of paper over a comb and blowing tunes, while across the street a bootblack would play a phonograph and beat out the rhythm on his customer's shoes. One night, a young clerk named Dick Slevin came out of the Butler Brothers Store with a kazoo and hummed along with the music. McKenzie crossed the street and joined in. Slevin knew a man named Jack Bland who played the banjo,

Below: A classic jam session on stage. Left to right; Ray Mayer (piano), Bobby Sherwood (trumpet), Phil Layton (trombone), Sidney Bechet (clarinet), Bert Edwards (bass) and Marty Marsala (drums).

Left: Earl 'Fatha' Hines conducts his orchestra during a 1940 session.

Below: Chicago native Benny Goodman, who attended Lewis Institute with drummer Dave Tough.

and soon the three of them were playing together. They went as a novelty act with Gene Rodemich's band and found themselves in Chicago. There bandleader Isham Jones got them a recording date, and their record 'Arkansaw Blues' and 'Blue Blues' sold over a million copies. McKenzie was hooked, and went on to form his own jazz band.

Leon Bismarck Beiderbecke was born in Davenport, Iowa, on 10 March 1903. Bix was never actually a person; he was a living legend. Nothing which has been invented about this round-eyed, eager-faced youngster with the mousy hair and the marvelous ear is as accurately symbolic as the everyday things he did. Without effort, he personified jazz; by natural selection he devoted himself to the outstanding characteristics of the music he loved. He was obsessed with it; he drove away all other things – food, sleep, women, ambition, vanity, desire. He played the cornet and the piano, and that was all, and actually his cornet playing was all wrong. He had no lip and his fingering was off – he was just the greatest. When he was sick, the Paul White-man orchestra kept an empty chair for him; when he died in 1931, no one was glad and many wept.

As a child, when he became tall enough to reach the piano keyboard, he was picking out tunes. He could play the melody of 'The Second Hungarian Rhapsody' when he was three years old. He did take piano lessons, but he didn't learn to read music. Then he heard jazz on the riverboats that came to Davenport in the summer and fell in love with Louis

Above: Benny Goodman, 'The King of Swing,' and his band in the late 1930s. In the top row are Gene Krupa (left, wearing hat) on drums and Harry James (second from left) on trumpet.

Opposite: Alson Skinner Clark's evocative painting *Coffee House*, painted in 1906.

Armstrong's style. He bought a cornet and taught himself to play – never mind the unorthodox fingering and the weak lip, he developed a round, full tone which was a wonder and a delight to all who heard him.

For a brief time (1921–2) he attended Lake Forest Academy in Chicago, winning prizes in music and flunking everything else. Every night he would duck out of school to play his cornet with dance orchestras on one-night stands up and down the North Shore, until his headmaster, convinced that Bix was wasting his time in school, released him in May of 1922. He listened to the jazz bands in Chicago, and when the players knew him and had heard him, they often asked him to sit in. He jobbed around with small pickup bands throughout the Midwest until 1923, when Dick Voynow, a piano player, organized a band called The Wolverines. They made records for Gennett, a small recording studio in Richmond, Indiana. Hoagy Carmichael, who was a student at Indiana University at the time, heard the records and brought the Wolverines to IU in the spring of 1924. After eight return visits on eight successive weekends, the Bix Beiderbecke legend had begun. The Wolverines took their place as one of the

great white jazz bands. Their records were a sensation. Bix was on his way.

Still the youngsters were hanging out on the South Side. Condon said of those times that the midnight air at 35th Street and Calumet Avenue was so full of music that if you held up an instrument the air would play it. Krupa, Wettling and Tough were watching Baby Dodds; Goodman and Marsala were watching Jimmy Noone; Spanier was watching Oliver and Louis Armstrong; and everyone was watching such great pianists as Teddy Weatherford, Thomas 'Fats' Waller and Earl 'Fatha' Hines.

These kids had no business being out so late at night – they were so young. Benny Goodman had been able to join the musician's union when he was only 12 years old, and Dave Tough was admitted when he was a mature 13. But sometimes the great ones would let the kids in after hours, and the boys began to lug their instruments with them. Once in a while lightning would strike. Armstrong would shout to Wettling, 'Now bring in that load of coal, George,' and the blond youngster would pound away at the drums. Somehow all of them got through high school.

Left: Poster by Oscar Rabe Hanson from 1923, one of a series depicting destinations which could be reached by the elevated railroad.

Right: The prosperity of the early twenties helped encourage vacation trips but swimsuit styles remained demure. This poster is by Hazel Urgelles and dates from 1925.

The Parks
by
THE ELEVATED LINES

Left: A further 1923 advert for the elevated railroad, poster by Helen Urgelles:

Right (all four): The new consumerism of the 1920s helped inspire a great increase in advertising output. This selection comprises, *top left,* a 1923 advert for brassieres, *top right,* a 1926 *Vogue* feature, and *both lower,* 1919 cosmetic advertising. At *lower left* the illustration shows the South Shore Country Club, Chicago.

Model Brassières Corset-Brassières
FOR THE CORRECT "SIL-U-ETTE"
Small up-lift bandeau type. In beautiful Etamine, lovely silks and satins, especially adapted for evening wear. $1.50 to $5.00.
Model Corset-Brassieres, four garter and two garter types. Made in finest materials. $1.50 to $7.50.
With what ease the costumes of some fortunate women seem to gain the universal eye of approval!
And yet, for the moulding and repression necessary to Fashion's decree, reliance on a fitting foundation such as Model affords, will give almost any woman this distinction.
Extra wide bandeau types in many charming materials. $1.00 to $5.00.
For sale everywhere. Send for illustrated booklet.
Model Brassière Co.
Dept. A
London • 200 Fifth Avenue, New York • Paris
Largest exclusive brassiere manufacturer in the world

VOGUE
Misses' Frock No. 8704
The front pleats of this canton crêpe frock are stitched to yoke depth and again at a low waistline. There is a double, turned-over collar, a plain back, and set-in sleeves tucked at the wrist. Designed for sizes 14 to 20 years
Misses' Frock No. 8706
Two tones of jersey combine in this frock. The overblouse has an applied front section, and belt sections slip through slashes and button. The separate skirt, on a lining, is pleated in front only. Designed for sizes 14 to 20 years
Misses' Frock No. 8705
The skirt of this cashmere frock has an inverted pleat and is joined to the blouse in a pointed line. An inserted vest with a small rolled collar, a narrow belt, and a straight back are other details. Designed for sizes 14 to 20 years
YOUTHFUL FROCKS OF SMART SIMPLICITY

The South Shore Country Club, Chicago
A COUNTRY club near a great city offers a constant succession of important functions. Often women must go directly from the "galleries" at the links or courts to the verandas or assembly rooms of the club. La Dorine in the handbag enables them to make this trying transition with confidence. La Dorine is applied so quickly, it adheres so perfectly, it harmonizes so exactly with the natural coloring of the skin that every trace of dust, heat or exertion disappears at once. An X-ray of the vanity bags at any smart club would show you La Dorine in most of them.
LA DORINE
The Imported Compact Powder from Paris
WHAT IS YOUR COLORING? Send description of your hair, eyes and complexion with 25c in stamps, and we will send two miniature compactes, La Dorine and one of Dorin's Rouges. Also booklet reproducing, in full color, seven exquisite types of beauty with directions for choosing the correct compactes for each type.
Or for 10c in stamps we will send the booklet with generous samples of La Dorine and Dorin's Rouge en poudre instead of the compactes.
LA DORINE comes in four shades to harmonize with every complexion— Blanche, Naturelle, Rosee and Rachel. Dorin's Compact Rouges are in a variety of natural tones of which Rouge Brunette and Rouge Framboise are the favorites. Large dressing table size, $1.00.
For arms and shoulders, use the Companion Powder, La Dorine en poudre. Box $1.00.
For your protection: Dorin's Preparations are sold only in containers marked "DORIN, PARIS"
F. R. ARNOLD & COMPANY Importers 7 WEST TWENTY-SECOND STREET, NEW YORK

MARY GARDEN
PERFUME
—la toilette de la Parisienne au bain de mer—
Mary Garden
Perfume
imparts its entrancing fragrance to the perfect
COLD CREAM
to the soft clinging
FACE POWDER
and to the delightfully refreshing
TOILET TALCUM
Rigaud
PARIS

Left: Favorite entertainments during the inter-war years were the barnstormers and air races.

Right: Despite Prohibition one could still enjoy the bright lights downtown, courtesy of the Elevated Lines.

Overleaf: Aspects of the prosperity of the 1920s and the marketing of the new technology being made available to the mass market. *(Top row left to right)* magazine of the South Shore Country Club, Chicago; 1919 hosiery ad; 1926 Chrysler; 1929 Cadillac. *(Bottom row)* 1926 radio; 1921 radiators; 1923 women's styles; 1924 Fords.

"BOUL MICH" *by the* ELEVATED LINES

south shore country club magazine

Hose as Shapely as the Curves of the Figure

THE translucent shimmer of Luxite Hosiery half reveals and half conceals. Its texture is so wonderfully soft and silken you can draw a Luxite silk stocking through your finger ring. Luxite launders beautifully because these hose contain no adulterations whatever—nothing but super-fine materials and pure dyes. Naturally Luxite Hosiery wears long and always looks beautiful.

Women's Silk Faced, $1.10; Pure Thread Japanese Silk, $1.30 to $2.25. Other styles, 55c. upward.
Men's Silk Faced, 65c.; Pure Thread Japanese Silk, 85c. and $1.10. Other Styles, 35c. up. Children's, 55c. up
If your favorite store cannot supply you, please write for illustrated book and price list.

LUXITE TEXTILES, Inc., 670 Fowler Street, Milwaukee, Wis.
Makers of High Grade Hosiery Since 1875

New York   Chicago

After theater— home *for the best dance music!*

RADIOLA 30 is "lighting socket radio" that is *tried · tested · perfected*

POWER reception with no batteries is the "new thing in radio" that you hear so much about. But through it is new, it has been tested and perfected, and you need not take chances on an untried purchase. RCA has been ahead of this day by nearly a year. And the Radiola 30 has had time to be thoroughly "road-tested."

It is in thousands of the finest homes. Its principles have been endorsed and adopted by Victor and Brunswick. It has power—and it's real! You can turn the music down

when the talk runs gaily. Or turn it up to full orchestra volume for a dance. It is natural and true no matter at what volume. It has a reserve of power—more than you will need tonight—and you'll never hear a

crash on the grand finale of a symphony.

Radiola 30 draws its power from the house wires, and takes no more care than an electric lamp! After theater, drive some for the best dance music, and tune in. End the evening with a perfect bit of supper, and music right from the night clubs. Even the big bass drum comes through—even the frenzied fingering of those high piano runs. Music is music and jazz is jazz, and it's *there* real in volume and in tone—with a Radiola 30.

Radiola 30, with the super-heterodyne with power speaker beautifully enclosed ... and superbly real in tone ... Complete, $575.
Slightly higher West of the Rockies.
RCA's California prices ...

RCA–Radiola

MADE · BY · THE · MAKERS · OF · THE · RADIOTRON

RADIO CORPORATION OF AMERICA · NEW YORK · CHICAGO · SAN FRANCISCO

Too rich to care— but he *did* care just the same

HE is one of the very rich men of the United States; his name is familiar to the newspaper readers of two continents.

Why should he care whether his coal bills are a third too large? But he did care just the same.

In remodeling his town house, he ordered the old-fashioned boiler taken out and an IDEAL TYPE A HEAT MACHINE installed. A 30% investment, tax exempt, seemed to him too good to lose!

Your Heating Contractor, or one of our Engineers, will examine your heating system and report without the slightest obligation to you. In all fairness to yourself, have this examination made; and remember let us send you the letters of testimonial from in various parts of the country who have installed the IDEAL TYPE A HEAT MACHINE and are now getting into the bank every year a third of what they used to put into the fire.

Merely ask your secretary to send your name on your business letterhead today.

IDEAL Type "A" Heat Machine

SOUTH MICHIGAN AVENUE
DEPT. 36, CHICAGO, ILL.

AMERICAN RADIATOR COMPANY

BRANCHES AND SHOWROOMS
IN ALL LARGE CITIES

Makers of the famous IDEAL Boilers and American Radiators

THE Chrysler Imperial "80" is built not simply for those who demand the best—but for those who *know* the best when they find it. As such the Imperial "80" possesses new and superlative qualities—in speed, power, smoothness, riding and driving ease, richness of upholstery and appointment—which the most glorious traditions have been unable to impart to the finest cars of yesterday.

CHRYSLER SALES CORPORATION, DETROIT, MICHIGAN
CHRYSLER CORPORATION OF CANADA, LIMITED, WINDSOR, ONT.

The Supreme Interpretation of Chrysler Standardized Quality

The Chrysler plan of Quality Standardization differs from, and is superior to, ordinary manufacturing practice and methods, because it demands fixed and inflexible quality standards which enforce the same scrupulously close limits—the same rigid rule of engineering exactness—the same absolute accuracy and precision of alignment and assemblage—in the measurement, the machining and the manufacturing of every part, practice and process in four lines of Chrysler cars—"50", "60", "70" and Imperial "80"—so that each individual car shall be the Supreme Value in its own class.

Ten body styles, priced from $2,495 to $3,595, f. o. b. Detroit, subject to current Federal excise tax.

CHRYSLER IMPERIAL "80"

CHRYSLER MODEL NUMBERS MEAN MILES PER HOUR

cadillac

*RADIANT NEW SMARTNESS
NEW HANDLING EASE
NEW SAFETY*

PROBABLY no introduction of new motor-car models has ever been so fraught with significance for the woman who drives her own car as this autumn's presentation of the newest and most highly polished Cadillac . . . These brilliant new Cadillac Models are deliberately designed so that women who are entitled to drive a car of commanding presence may freely do so without fear or fatigue . . . The Syncro-Mesh Silent-Shift Transmission and the Safety-Mechanical Four-Wheel Brakes, which last year revolutionized gear shifting and braking, and both of which are protected by basic patents and are, therefore, not available in any other car, have been raised to new heights of efficiency and ease of operation . . . A new harmonized steering system makes these cars amazingly easy to handle both in city traffic and in cross-country driving . . . The adjustable front seats are even more easily adjusted than in the past . . . In all the new Cadillac windows, doors and windshields, the indispensable protection of non-shatterable Security-Plate Glass is standard equipment . . . The new Cadillac Fisher and Fleetwood bodies add the crowning touch of a quiet elegance and quality in coachcraft in comparison with which other coachwork appears disturbingly inadequate.

CADILLAC MOTOR CAR COMPANY, DIVISION OF GENERAL MOTORS, DETROIT, MICHIGAN

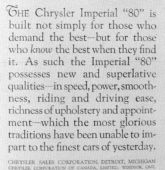

A Complete Summer Outfit at Very Moderate Cost

Everyone will see that these four models are pretty—smart—distinctive, but who under the sun would realize how inexpensive they are; never a man in the whole world, and very few women.

Both Pamico Cloth and Serpentine Crepe are manufactured by the Pacific Mills—the world's largest makers of printed, dyed and bleached cottons. They are sold by nearly every retailer in dry goods. If you do not find just what you desire, write Mrs. Charles R. Insull, 24 Federal St., Boston, for samples.

PACIFIC MILLS

*Lawrence, Mass., Dover, N. H.,
Columbia, S. C.,*

Her habit of measuring time in terms of dollars gives the woman in business keen insight into the true value of a Ford closed car for her personal use.

This car enables her to conserve minutes, to expedite her affairs, to widen the scope of her activities. Its low first cost, long life and inexpensive operation and upkeep convince her that it is a sound investment value.

And it is such a pleasant car to drive that it transforms the business call which might be an interruption into an enjoyable episode of her busy day.

TUDOR SEDAN, $580   FORDOR SEDAN, $685   COUPE, $525   *All prices f. o. b. Detroit*

Ford CLOSED CARS

Left: French style on show in Chicago in 1933.

Right: Ivan Albright's *Self Portrait at E Division Street* (1935).

Below: The National Recovery Administration helped sponsor parades in Chicago in the early years of Franklin Roosevelt's presidency but was struck down by the Supreme Court in 1935 as unconstitutional.

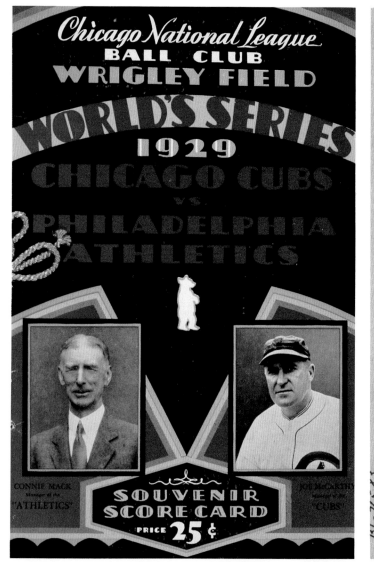

Above & left: Great days for the Cubs and all their fans at Wrigley Field.

Right: The winter game too had its moments courtesy of the Fighting Irish of Notre Dame and the South Shore Railroad.

INJUN SUMMER

(Copyright: 1912: By John T. McCutcheon. Reprinted here by general request. The original of this cartoon hangs in the museum of the Chicago Historical society.)

Yep, sonny, this is sure enough Injun summer. Don't know what that is, I reckon, do you?

Well, that's when all the homesick Injuns come back to play. You know, a long time ago, long afore yer granddaddy was born even, there used to be heaps of Injuns around here—thousands—millions, I reckon, far as that's concerned. Reg'lar sure 'nough Injuns—none o' yer cigar store Injuns, not much. They wuz all around here—right here where you're standin'.

Don't be skeered—hain't none around here now, leastways no live ones. They been gone this many a year.

They all went away and died, so they ain't no more left.

But every year, 'long about now, they all come back, leastways their sperrits do. They're here now. You can see 'em off across the fields. Look real hard. See that kind o' hazy, misty look out yonder? Well, them's Injuns—Injun sperrits marchin' along an' dancin' in the sunlight. That's what makes that kind o' haze that's everywhere—it's jest the sperrits of the Injuns all come back. They're all around us now.

See off yonder; see them tepees? They kind o' look like corn shocks from here, but them's Injun tents, sure as you're a foot high. See 'em now?

Sure, I knowed you could. Smell that smoky sort o' smell in the air? That's the campfires a-burnin' and their pipes a-goin'.

Lots o' people say it's just leaves burnin', but it ain't. It's the campfires, an' th' Injuns are hoppin' 'round 'em t' beat the old Harry.

You jest come out here tonight when the moon is hangin' over the hill off yonder an' the harvest fields is all swimmin' in the moonlight, an' you can see the Injuns and the tepees jest as plain as kin be. You can, eh? I knowed you would after a little while.

Jever notice how the leaves turn red 'bout this time o' year? That's jest another sign o' redskins. That's when an old Injun sperrit gits tired dancin' an' goes up an' squats on a leaf t'rest. Why, I kin hear 'em rustlin' an' whisperin' an' creepin' 'round among the leaves all the time; an' ever' once'n a while a leaf gives way under some fat old Injun ghost and comes floatin' down to the ground. See—here's one now. See how red it is? That's the war paint rubbed off'n an Injun ghost, sure's you're born.

Purty soon all the Injuns'll go marchin' away agin, back to the happy huntin' ground, but next year you'll see 'em troopin' back—th' sky jest hazy with 'em and their campfires smolderin' away jest like they are now.

In 1922 the Chicago kids put together their first band, called the Blue Friars, named after the Friars' Inn Society Orchestra (which was the recording name for the New Orleans Rhythm Kings). The boys, ranging in age from 14 to 17, were: Jim Lannigan (piano and later bass), Jimmy MacPartland (cornet), Dick MacPartland (banjo and guitar), Lawrence 'Bud' Freeman (C-melody saxophone), Frank Teschmaker (violin and later alto saxophone), Dave North (piano) and, when they were needed, Dave Tough (drums) and Benny Goodman (clarinet).

They played a lot of gigs at the old White City Amusement Park at 63rd Street and South Park Avenue, which had two dance halls on the premises at the time. The band played its first summer at Lost Lake and were so successful that a promoter named O'Hare took them over and renamed them Husk O'Hare's Wolverines, with Floyd O'Brien joining them on trombone.

Their big competition was the original Wolverines, featuring Bix Beiderbecke wearing his four-button suit and his broken-peaked cap. He had previously begged the Blue Friars to let him join their band, but the Chicago boys thought that he had no class – he didn't know how to dress, and he seldom changed his underwear.

Still, the Chicago boys did admire the Wolverines. They would play their records and wait impatiently for Bix to hit town so that they could hear him on the piano and

take him to hear Bessie Smith. Bessie was the Empress of the Blues. She began her career singing for coins on Chattanooga street corners. In 1907, when she was 13 years old, she was discovered by Gertrude 'Ma' Rainey, one of the first great blues singers, while she was singing for $2.50 per week in tent shows. Bessie had a contralto voice of such power and range and tone, of such richness and adaptability, that there was no one to rival or imitate or follow her. She was unmatched. In the days before the Depression, blacks would stand in line all over the country to buy her records – 'Empty Bed Blues,' 'Careless Love,' 'Nobody Knows You When You're Down and Out' and 'Young Women's Blues.' She sang many of the blues written by Clarence Williams, the New Orleans piano player who migrated to Chicago, opened a music shop and became the publisher of his own songs.

In the beginning, Bessie Smith's rich, powerful, emotional vocal style was considered excessive by three different recording companies. She also lost points when, during a test recording, she stopped the band and announced she had to spit. It was that kind of earthiness that appealed to her fans. On stage, she was magnificent, graceful despite her six-foot, 200-pound frame.

It is no accident when a great singer also turns out to be a first-rate actress. Smith proved that in her appearance singing the title song in the film *St Louis Blues*.

She hit hard times in mid-life. Her seven-

Opposite: Cartoon by John McCutcheon, a regular contributor to the *Chicago Tribune.* McCutcheon, a native of Indiana, is best know for his cartoons of midwestern rural life.

Below: After his stint with the Goodman band, Gene Krupa formed his own organization.

year marriage to a former policeman (later her manager) broke up in 1930. Her drinking habit, begun in childhood, began to dominate her life. The Great Depression brought a decline in record sales. Radio, which was growing up, felt it could do without black performers. Bessie died in an automobile crash in Mississippi in 1937, but her musical legacy was incalculable. Billie Holliday and Mahalia Jackson, among other singers, claimed that Smith was the greatest influence on their careers.

Erskine Tate and his Vendome Syncopators played at the Vendome for most of the 1920s. The band had 15 pieces and played a solid two-hour-long concert between the showings of the feature film. At one time or another, many great musicians played with this band – Louis Armstrong, Freddie Keppard, Jubbo Smith, Earl 'Fatha' Hines, Fats Waller, Cass Simpson and Jimmy Bertrand. It was at the Vendome that Armstrong first put on a skit featuring the Reverend Satchelmouth, forever earning himself a nickname.

In the early years of Prohibition, one all-white band was extremely popular in Chicago

Below: Al Capone (left), because of his night club and speakeasy businesses, became a patron of the arts of jazz and swing. Here he is being greeted by Chicago Chief of Detectives John Stege in 1930, and apparently enjoying himself.

– The New Orleans Rhythm Kings. It was a good one. The band had been formed in New Orleans in 1919, and made early tours to Mobile, Alabama, and to Texas. It had played on the Strekfus Line riverboats and came to Chicago in 1920. Featuring Paul Mares on trumpet, George Brunies on trombone and Leon Rappolo on clarinet, it soon became the toast of the town.

The star of the New Orleans Rhythm Kings was Leon Rappolo. The driving force of the band was George Brunies. Both were from New Orleans and both were veterans of Storyville. Rappolo ran away from home when he was 14 and played in a band with Bee Palmer's act on the Orpheum Circuit. The police found him and sent him home. He worked then at the Halfway House in Storyville with Abbie Brunies, George's brother.

When the band was booked into the Cascades Ballroom on the North Side of Chicago, a strange thing happened. The piano at the Cascades was a half-tone off, confusing pianist Elmer Schoebel and resulting in such strange harmonies that the Kings became the most sought-after jazzmen in town and moved to Mike Fritzel's Friars' Club on the strength of their version of 'Wabash Blues.'

It was there that something happened that would become a common thing in the swing era of the 1930s and 1940s. At times Rappolo would play chorus after chorus on his clarinet, as the customers stopped dancing and crowded around the bandstand to listen. Fritzell begged Rappolo to stop so that the people could sit down and spend some money, but Rappolo couldn't control himself. So enchanted were the Rhythm Kings with Chicago life that after work, in the early dawn, they rode around for hours on the elevated trains.

Rappolo slowly went mad. He liked to lean against a telephone pole and improvise on his clarinet the rhythm he heard humming in the wires. When he became harmlessly insane, he returned to New Orleans and Abbie Brunies took him back into the band that played at the Halfway House and looked after him until he died.

Improvisation by adolescent white boys reared in polite homes was bound to be different from the conversational instrumentation of black men belonging to a minority of 13 million submerged in the freest nation on earth. It was a fresh expression, and a new voice. But unfortunately, jazz was not considered a proper profession for well-bred young white men. Band leaders who dispensed popular music were as disapproving as parents who revered Beethoven. The Austin High boys and their friends had to work in cabarets and speakeasies. Al Capone and his boys replaced the madams of Storyville as

Above: Left to right: Harry Barris, Bing Crosby and Al Rinker – Paul Whiteman's singing Rhythm Boys – who got into a scrape in Cicero, outside of Chicago, when they unwittingly accepted an invitation extended by the Capone mob.

sponsors for the new music. Playing in small groups, experimenting with techniques, the youngsters developed a style based on, but different from, the jazz of New Orleans. The beat was pushed and nervous, the tympani had the sound of urgent Indian drums, there was tenseness, almost frenzy, in the solo flights of the horns.

In the 1920s there used to be a little speakeasy at State and Lake Streets. It was in a cellar, had an upright piano, and served only cheap gin. But the musicians would hang out there after hours – both those from the jazz world and those from the big bands that played the Chicago Theater – to jam a little. Tommy and Jimmy Dorsey would drop in when they were in town, as would Ben Pollack and Paul Whiteman. One night Whiteman's three Rhythm Boys came over and listened to Bix until 7:30 AM (Bix was playing with Whiteman at the time, although he considered himself a prostitute). The Rhythm Boys consisted of Al Rinker, Harry Barris and Bing Crosby. A string of black sedans drove up in front of the speakeasy and Crosby explained to Bix, 'Some fellow wants us all to go out to Cicero and play at a party. I told him we would go.' They went to the

84

Greyhound Club in Cicero, where a sticky evil-looking person kept yelling at the band. Bix shouted to him to shut up or he'd punch him in the nose. The fellow shut up. Later Eddie Condon explained to Bix that he had been threatening 'Bottles' Capone, Big Al's brother.

By the late 1920s, Chicago style jazz had swept the country. The real jazzmen were

Right: The master of the jazz trumpet – Wingy Manone.

loyal to their music, but sometimes they had to eat, so they would go over to the schmaltz side for a time. For example, Wingy Manone once had to scrape together a band for a two-night stand at the world's foremost Palace of Schmaltz, the Aragon Ballroom on the North Side – a Spanish-Moorish cathedral to bad taste that was later to feature bands the likes of Wayne King's, Dick Jurgens' and Freddie Martin's. But when a jazz musician who happened to be at the Aragon that night came up to the bandstand and yelled, 'Take off the false whiskers, Wingy, I know you,' the band broke up in the middle of a waltz and ripped the roof off with 'Jazzin' Babies Blues.'

Wingy and his band's real roots were at My Cellar, at Randolph and Clark Streets – a favorite after-hours hangout. All the Chicago jazzmen came to sit in at one time or another with Wingy and his sidemen. In the late 1920s and early 1930s, the rage was the 'Battle of the Bands,' where two bands alternated. Whichever band got the most applause won. The greatest of all the battles of the bands was that between Wingy Manone's and Benny Goodman's bands at the Midway Gardens in Chicago. The two were friends and knew each other's repertoires. Wingy's band knew only 10 numbers, and when the Goodman band started first, they played all 10 of them. All Wingy could do was to play them all over again while the audience grumbled.

Nineteen thirty-three marked the first year of the Chicago World's Fair – 'A Century of Progress' – and all the music that was played there was schmaltz. The second year of the fair, only a spot called 'Harry's New York Bar' had jazz. But the man who owned a joint called 'The Brewery,' just outside the 23rd Street entrance to the fair, decided that if he were going to stay in business, he had to get a loud band to attract attention, so he hired Manone. Wingy blew them down, playing so loud that bands inside the fair were thrown out of tune. Ben Bernie was drowned out – he was playing nearest the entrance inside the fair. Jack Teagarden was also inside playing schmaltz for $90 per week. After hearing Manone off in the distance, he took his trombone to The Brewery, saying, 'You win' to Wingy, and finished the season with Manone at $60 per week.

About this time, Chicagoans were beginning to listen to another type of improvised music — gospel. And Mahalia Jackson was the first singer to make it profitable. Until she came along, gospel singing was seldom heard outside black churches.

Mahalia was born in 1911, the child of a part-time preacher, and grew up in New Orleans. She was not permitted to listen to anything but gospel, which partly explains why she never sang anything else. 'Gospel singing is a heart feeling,' she once said. 'It's also got His love, and that's what I've got to sing if I'm going to sing at all.'

Professional singing wasn't to come until she was in her twenties. After graduation from elementary school, she got a job as a laundress and maid. At 16 she moved to Chicago, where she worked as a hotel maid and in a factory while attending beautician's school. Mahalia opened up a beauty shop, then a flower shop, then bought some real estate. She began singing with a gospel group in her Chicago church and made her first record, 'God Gonna Separate the Wheat from the Tares,' in 1934. Ten years later, her records would be selling in the millions.

The last great year of Chicago jazz was 1939. That February, the fans could hear Wingy Manone at the Three Deuces on State Street, where Jimmy MacPartland and Art Tatum were doing singles upstairs. Gene Krupa was at the College Inn at the Hotel Sherman, Stuff Smith was at the LaSalle Hotel, Bob Crosby's Bobcats were at the Blackhawk Restaurant and Fletcher Henderson was at the Grand Terrace.

Those who liked other forms of popular music could catch the stage shows at the Chicago, State-Lake and Oriental Theaters. Or they could go to supper clubs like the

Left: A corner of the dance floor in the Aragon Ballroom, that Moorish nightmare at 1106 West Lawrence Avenue where big swing bands used to hold sway.

Chez Paree to hear the contrasting styles of two women who were to become the singing darlings of the Windy City.

Sophie Tucker, the 'Last of the Red Hot Mammas,' was born in 1884, as she said, 'on the road' in Russia. Her mother was on her way to join Tucker's father in America, where

Below: Benny Goodman and his band played at the Congress Casino in the Congress Hotel on Michigan Avenue in 1935. Gene Krupa was with him on drums even then.

Right: Tommy Dorsey (left) had a lot of talent in his swing band in the late 1930s. Frank Sinatra (fourth from left) was his male singer. The other four people in the photo were The Modernaires, his singing group, one of whom went on to make quite a name for herself, too – Jo Stafford.

Opposite left: The great pianist and orchestra leader, Count Basie.

Opposite right: Isham Jones, whose dance band was a Chicago favorite in the early 1930s.

Below: Earl 'Fatha' Hines (left) leads his band – 1940.

he had fled to avoid military service. Although her family name was Kalish, Tucker grew up as Sophie Abuza. Her father, fearful of being apprehended by Russian authorities, had taken the identity of a deceased Italian friend.

Her father owned a restaurant in Hartford, Connecticut, where Sophie occasionally sang, but she was forbidden to enter show business. On the pretext of taking a vacation, Tucker set off for New York in 1906 to become a singer. Tucker sang for her suppers. She won a part in an amateur show and was required to wear blackface because the theater manager thought her 'too big and ugly.'

She sang between the acts at a Ziegfeld Follies production, but was fired because the stars resented her eager reception. So she joined the Morris vaudeville circuit.

Tucker's nickname stemmed from her choice of *double entendre* numbers. They dealt with sex, she said, not vice. She popularized such songs as 'Mother (the Word That Means the World to Me)' and 'Yiddisha Mama,' and all Chicago was flocking to hear her sing her theme, 'Some of These Days.'

The other idol of Chicago was 'The Incomparable' Hildegarde. She was the 'Continental Chanteuse' from Milwaukee who parlayed 'Darling, *Je Vous Aime Beaucoup*' into an international musical identity. She made her show business debut in Springfield, Massachusetts, as a member of 'Gerry and Her Baby Grands,' four young ladies dressed in Colonial costumes and wearing powdered wigs who played white baby grand pianos

equipped with keyboards that lit up red, white and blue when they burst into 'The Stars and Stripes Forever.' She auditioned for this group by playing 'Twelfth Street Rag.' When Chicagoans watched her act at the elegantly appointed Drake Hotel, they were watching something regal and they loved every minute of it.

But swing was coming in. Chicago had long been fond of this style of musicianship – inventive, but less driving than jazz – with its improvisations written down on a page of music, only the riffs being invented on the spot. In the area of what would be known as swing, Chicago's favorite band was that of Isham Jones, who arrived in town in the early 1920s, opening with his band, his saxophone and his piano at the Old Green Mill. But his true home was at the Hotel Sherman, run by Ernie Byfield, before he switched to the Pump Room at the Ambassador East. The premier restaurateur of Chicago, Byfield claimed to have invented the club sandwich. Jones stayed at the College Inn for six years, sometimes playing his own songs, such as 'Swinging Down the Lane,' 'It Had to Be You' and 'I'll See You in My Dreams.'

Chicagoans had other places to go to hear swing. There was the Chez Paree, the night club at Fairbanks Court and Ontario Street, where anybody who was anybody in music came to perform. There were also the Boulevard Room at the Stevens Hotel (now the Conrad Hilton), The College Inn at the Hotel Sherman, the Trianon Ballroom at 62nd Street and Cottage Grove Avenue, which was

Opposite: Teddy Wilson was a pianistic genius.

Right: 'The Incomparable Hildegarde,' who sold out every performance when she hit town to appear in a night club.

opened in 1922. This dance hall had crystal chandeliers, and such schmaltzy bands as Kay Kyser, Ted Weems and Jan Garber were to get their first big breaks there. Indeed, when Rudolph Valentino danced the tango at the Trianon on 18 February 1923, there were 6000 fans watching him do it, and thousands more outside, hoping for a glimpse of their hero.

The Drake Hotel had its Silver Forest Room, where Hal Kemp and Fred Waring held forth, and where Phil Spitalny introduced his all-girl orchestra featuring Evelyn and her Magic Violin.

But it was good old Chicago boy Benny Goodman who became the 'King of Swing.' The crowds shouted 'Get off Benny, swing it,' and 'Feed it to me Gene [Krupa].' Those were the jitterbugs or alligators who gave us new words for our vocabularies: in the groove, give me skin, boogie-woogie, jam session, killer diller. Closely behind Goodman were to come Artie Shaw, Tommy and Jimmy Dorsey, Count Basie, Teddy Wilson, Larry Clinton, and a couple of holdovers – Louis Armstrong and Jack Teagarden.

Right: Libby Holman, another favorite in Chicago in the 1930s, was a night club singer specializing in the blues.

Below: Morton Downey was a sellout in Chicago night clubs, too, with his pure tenor crooning.

OPERA AND SYMPHONY

Chicago opera during the Glamour Years was as good as any in the world. The Chicago Opera Association held sway from 1915 to 1922, then changed its name to the Chicago Civic Opera Company. The Civic collapsed in 1932 because of the Great Depression, to be revived as the Chicago Grand Opera Company for one season. Then a company called the Stadium Opera Company tried to perform in the Chicago Stadium, but that arena was better suited to the Chicago Black Hawks hockey games, and the company died. In 1935 the Chicago City Opera Company was formed, and this lasted into the 1940s with short seasons in the Civic Opera House. But they were great seasons, featuring such luminaries as Rose Bampton, Kirsten Flagstad, Helen Jepson, Grace Moore, Lili Pons, Beniamino Gigli, Giuseppe Martinelli, James Melton, Igor Kipnis, Ezio Pinza and Lawrence Tibbett.

During the 1920s, Mary Garden was the toast of the Chicago Civic Opera Company. She was the star. She could sing. She could act. She had the voice of an angel and the looks to match. Born in Scotland and raised in Chicago, she was a breezy, gabby home-grown product, and for 20 years she was the personification of operatic glamour in Chicago.

Once she was asked to go to the Chicago Mercantile Exchange to auction off a few tickets to the opera. Garden was always happy to be in male company, and went into her sales job. But no sooner had she started than a man with long gray hair and shabby clothes tried to shoot her. He was stopped by a policeman before he could pull the trigger, and when asked why he had tried to shoot the beloved Mary, he said, 'She talks too much.' Much of musical Chicago considered the man a martyr, and Garden's colleagues in the opera were almost unanimous in pointing out that if the would-be assassin were crazy enough to want to shut Mary Garden up, then the entire personnel of the opera should also be put into an asylum.

Mary Garden, who was a good friend of Billy Sunday, the baseball player turned ranting evangelist who ran a mission on South State Street, was named director of the company in 1921. However, she chose her own title, and insisted on being called 'Directa.' She sang, she selected the operas to be performed (choosing choice roles for herself), she supervised the performers. She demoted Gino Marinuzzi from artistic director to conductor, and he immediately resigned.

Garden's selection of operas was a bit unusual, but in truth, Chicago was the most sophisticated opera town in the world. Where else could one see Ruggiero Leoncavallo's *Zaza* except in Chicago? Of course Garden had a feud with Ganna Walska, who was supposed to star in the vehicle, and Walska walked out of the rehearsals.

Mary Garden also had the nerve to put on the world premiere of Sergei Prokofiev's *The Love of Three Oranges* on 30 December 1921. This esoteric opera starred Nina Koshetz in her American debut as the Fata Morgana, and the composer was on hand to conduct. In 1922 Prokofiev and the entire Chicago Opera Company were transported east to perform the New York premiere of the opera on 14 February. It was not to be presented again in the United States until the New York City Center Opera revived it in 1950.

Mary Garden lasted a year as 'Directa.' After that, the man with the money, Samuel Insull, the financier, began insisting that

Previous pages: A crowd watching the arrival of society folk at the opening performance at Chicago's Civic Opera House in 1929. The opera on 5 November of that year was Giuseppe Verdi's *Aida*.

Below: The celebrated Mary Garden was so striking that she dominated the stage in every role she performed. Here she is elegantly gowned for the title role in Jules Massenet's *Sappho*.

During those years, Feodor Chaliapin was lured to Chicago to sing the title role in Arrigo Boïto's *Mephistophele* – an extremely rare event, since the opera had been unfairly eclipsed by Charles Gounod's *Faust*, which had the same plot. Indeed, it would be years before the opera was heard again in the United States.

Chicago opera fans were also applauding

Far left: The Bible-thumping revivalist and former professional baseball player Billy Sunday, who ran a mission on South State Street, was a friend of Mary Garden.

Left: Mary Garden strikes a seductive and menacing pose after she instigates the beheading of John the Baptist, in Richard Strauss' *Salome.*

things be run in a more business-like way. Garden stayed on as the star, however, and was to have her most glamorous years later. It turned out that the years of the Insull regime were good ones, especially since the Chicago Opera Company paid more for singers than the New York Metropolitan Opera Company did, and Chicago was able to get the top stars.

At the time, the old Auditorium where the Chicago Opera Company and later the Chicago Civic Opera Company performed was called the 'Ebbets Field of Opera.' Almost anything could happen there. Once, a couple of supers, who had figured in some of the crowd scenes in Giuseppe Verdi's *Aida*, through for the night, started out of the theater in their street clothes, then thought of taking a shortcut. They crossed the stage, not knowing that the curtain had gone up, and walked across the bed of the Nile River through a host of Egyptian soldiers. It was not unusual to see a Delilah fall downstairs, lunatics rush onstage to be fended off by Romeo's prop sword, bombers threatening to blow up the theater. A tenor was once arrested for trapping and eating pigeons that were roosting outside his hotel-room window.

Ermanno Wolf-Ferrari's *The Secret of Suzanne* is a modest one-act opera that tells the story of Count Gill and Countess Suzanna. The Count grows jealous when he keeps smelling the odor of tobacco smoke when he comes home. After a lot of foolishness, he finds out that it is she who has been smoking in the house. Anti-smoking elements of the Chicago population tried to get the opera barred from the company's repertoire.

such bits of esoterica as Nikolai Rimsky-Korsakov's *The Snow Maiden* (under its original title of *Sniegurotchka*). Other little-performed operas in the repertoire were Giaccomo Puccini's *The Girl of the Golden West*, Carl Maria von Weber's *Der Freischütz* and Giuseppi Verdi's *La Forza del Destino* – none of them being performed at any other opera house at that time. Mary Garden picked herself to star in a couple of other obscure operas – Victor Herbert's *Natoma* (which was not a good idea) and Jules Massinet's *Werther* (which was).

During this period, Marion Claire, Lotte Lehmann and Jennie Tourel all made their American debuts in Chicago, as did the future actor Orson Welles, who had walk-ons as a small child and once even played Cio-Cio-San's illegitimate child, Trouble, in Giaccomo Puccini's *Madama Butterfly*.

In 1929 the company moved into Samuel Insull's monument to himself, the Civic Opera House, on North Wacker Drive. It was a huge building, containing the Civic Theater, thousands of offices, and the opera house itself, which had a 14-story-high stage

and could seat 3600. When the season closed in 1929 at the old theater, with a farewell-to-the-Auditorium performance of Charles Gounod's *Romeo and Juliet* (the same opera that had opened the theater in 1889), the audience joined in a rendition of 'Home, Sweet Home' (Adelina Patti had sung the same song at the opening so long ago). The dedication of the Civic Opera House was held on 4 November 1929, only 11 days after the Stock Market Crash.

There was much activity on another front – symphonic music – too. Theodore Thomas had founded the Chicago Symphony in 1886, when it was hard to persuade musicians to come to Chicago, or to stay there. The long winters and the dampness indoors didn't do much for a delicate musical instrument, or for a human body, for that matter. But Thomas had been quoted as saying 'I would go to hell if they would give me a permanent orchestra.' Who knows what he thought when he gave his first concert in Chicago in Orchestra Hall before the plaster was dry.

Still, the orchestra was a pioneer group. Even in 1915, there were a mere 17 symphony

Below: Swindler though he was, Samuel Insull was the guiding genius behind the Chicago Civic Opera. It was he who caused the new Civic Opera House to be built.

Above: Lotte Lehmann, the great soprano, was a favorite of Chicago opera fans.

Above left: Feodor Chaliapin in 1923. The great Russian basso was lured to Chicago to sing Arrigo Boîto's *Mephistophele*.

Left: Lehmann as Elisabeth in Richard Wagner's *Tannhäuser*.

Far left: Orchestra Hall on Michigan Avenue – the home of the Chicago Symphony Orchestra.

Daguerre
Chicago

Above: Lucretia Bori, another Civic Opera stalwart – in Georges Bizet's *Carmen.*

Above right: Giovanni Martinelli at Ravinia as Tristan in Richard Wagner's *Tristan und Isolde.*

Opposite: Claudia Muzio as she appeared in the title role of Giacomo Puccini's *Tosca* at Ravinia.

orchestras in the United States. By 1939 the number had risen to 270 – and Chicago was one of the old stand-bys. In the Glamour Years, the Chicago Symphony was ruled by Frederick Stock, a martinet and a pretty fair musician. This was not a great symphony, but it certainly was more than adequate. Who cared that they were only hired to record overtures on 12-inch single shellac records? The orchestra educated people. They would often give free children's concerts, and you could count on Stock's turning to the audience of moppets to say, 'Everybody cough – blow your noses, and then we'll play.'

In the 1920s, as it is today, the North Shore's biggest and most popular community event was the Ravinia Festival in the town of Highland Park. Ravinia Park was to Chicago what Tanglewood was to Boston or the Hollywood Bowl to Los Angeles. It was the summer home of the Chicago Symphony, of course, but music lovers could also hear Walter Damrosch and the New York Sym-

phony, or attend concerts by the Minneapolis Symphony under Eugene Ormandy. One summer Ted Shawn and Ruth St Denis were the dancers in residence. During another summer, Ben Greet's Shakespearian Company was performing. In short, Ravinia became the Bayreuth of America.

By the mid-1920s there was at Ravinia an opera company in residence that was the envy of the world. It featured such singers as Claudia Muzio, Edith Mason, Antonio Scotti, Lucretia Bori, Elisabeth Rethberg, Giovanni Martinelli and Tito Schipa. And, in the time-honored way so typical of Chicago opera, they often performed exotica. For example, there was Manuel De Falla's *La Vida Breve*, Modest Moussorgsky's *Boris Godunov*, Franco Leoni's *L'Oracolo* and Leroux's *Marouf*. Because of the Great Depression, however, the opera performances ceased in 1932, and by 1936 Chicagoans had to settle for just six weeks of the Chicago Symphony Orchestra plus one week of chamber music.

BOOKS AND PERIODICALS

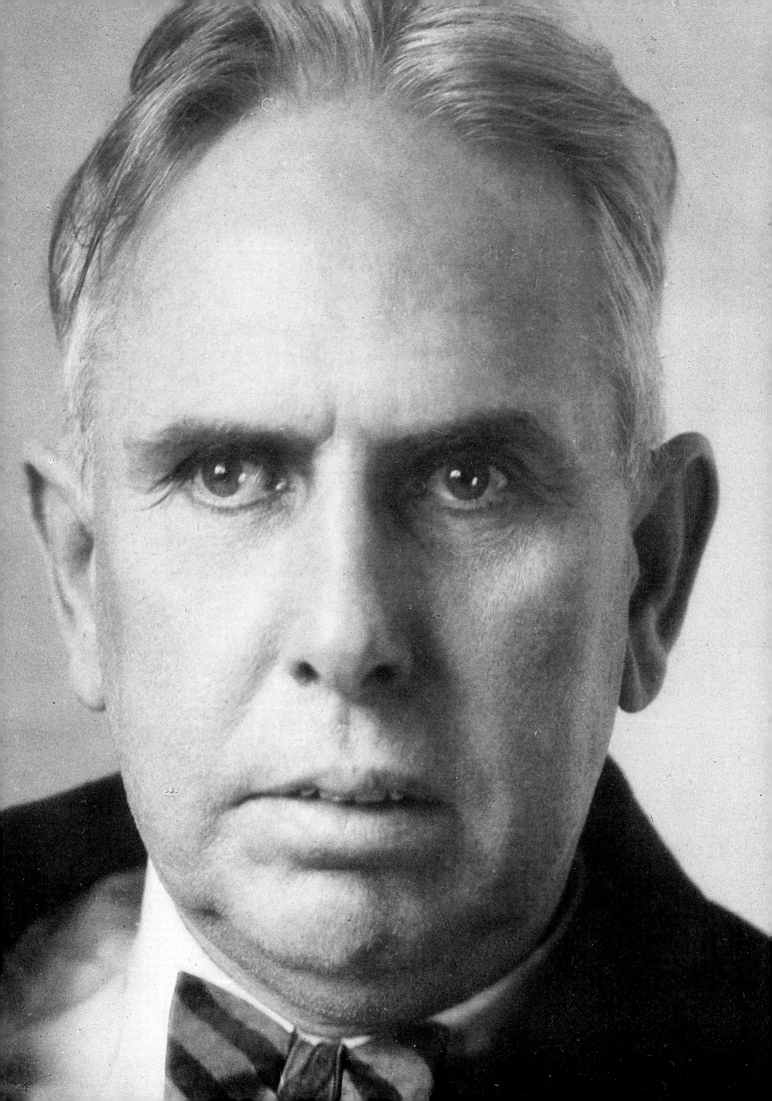

Just as it was a mecca for jazz musicians, Chicago was a mecca for writers – some were native born and others came from all over the country to find inspiration in this literary city that had nurtured such greats as Frank Norris, whose novels, such as *McTeague, The Octopus* and *The Pit*, concentrated on the physical, the sordid and the violent; George Ade, the humorist and playwright, best known for his *Fables in Slang*; and Finley Peter Dunne, the humorist and creator of 'Mr Dooley.'

The writers living in Chicago during the Glamour Years could make up a Who's Who of American letters. Carl Sandburg was there, working for the Chicago *Daily News*, writing his poetry and playing his guitar in his free time. The monumental Theodore Dreiser was writing his voluminous and bitterly realistic novels (his most famous, *An American Tragedy*, appeared in 1925). After Dreiser's death, Howard Mumford wrote, 'The death of Theodore Dreiser removes from the American scene something primary, brooding and enormous, it is as if a headland crumbled and slid into the sea.'

Upton Sinclair was working on his books in Chicago. Sinclair was a novelist and mis-cellaneous author known for his affiliation with Socialism, and his writings dealt with pacifism, political corruption, social problems, perversions of justice, economic inequality and the like. He was most famous for *The Jungle*, in which he exposed the criminal conditions in the Chicago Union Stock Yards – conditions of filth, contamination and miserable treatment of the people who worked there. One critic said, 'Sinclair aimed for the reader's heart but hit his stomach.' His Lanny Budd novels, and there were eight of them, were described as 'a daydream at a newsreel.'

Edna Ferber, the novelist, short-story writer and playwright, cut her literary teeth in Chicago, publishing *So Big* in 1924.

Sherwood Anderson was associated with the Chicago group, too. He became famous for his realistic portrayal of life in the small towns of the American Midwest, and hit the big time with *Winesburg, Ohio* in 1919. Edgar Lee Masters, the poet best known for his *Spoon River Anthology*, which gave a dramatic and realistic portrait of life in the Midwest, was originally trained as a lawyer. This Chicago literary genius wrote in the tradition of E W Howe, Joseph Kirkland and Hamlin Garland, depicting the Midwest, and later twentieth-century America also, in a realistic, pessimistic and iconoclastic light. His aims in his best-known poetry were similar to those of Sherwood Anderson in prose.

Vachel Lindsay was a dear friend of Edgar Lee Masters. This poet, known for the vivid imagery and striking dramatic and auditory effects of his poetry, often read his own works from the lecture platform with theatrical gestures and intonation, in an effort to

Previous pages: Theodore Dreiser, (1871-1945) one of America's greatest novelists.

Below right: A caricature of the folk humorist George Ade (1866-1944).

Below: The major American poet and folksinger Carl Sandburg, as photographed by Edward Steichen in 1919.

cultivate a love of poetry in the people. His work dealt with American subjects and heroes, patriotism and mystic faith in nature and the soil. Lindsay was a striking personality who lived an adventurous life. During the first years of his career, he lectured on temperance and art in the winter and spent the summer as a vagabond, trading his poems for food and shelter.

Chicago's Floyd Dell became known for a number of novels dealing with post-war disillusionment, youth in the Jazz Age and the Bohemian life, the most popular being *Moon-Calf*. Maxwell Bodenheim, the poet and novelist, was known for the sardonic and iconoclastic nature of his writings and was a typical Bohemian of the 1920s. Vincent Starrett, an expert on the private life of Sherlock Holmes, was writing his verse, mysteries and non-fiction.

Francis Hackett was a Chicago critic, biographer and novelist. Westbrook Pegler, before he became a reactionary columnist, was a Chicago sports reporter. Richard Wright, the black novelist and short-story writer, known for his fictional studies of race problems and the black experience in the United States, published *Uncle Tom's Children* in 1938 and his monumental book *Native Son* in 1940.

Ben Hecht was a member of the Chicago group – a novelist, short-story writer, playwright and newspaperman, known for his eroticism and flamboyant Bohemianism, who wrote like a combination of Gautier, Huynmans and Dostoyevsky. He was passionately fond of Chicago, and two of his short-story collections were titled *1001 Afternoons in Chicago* and *Tales of Chicago Streets*. He

wrote several plays with Maxwell Bodenheim, then teamed up with Charles MacArthur, another Chicago playwright and newspaperman (who later married actress Helen Hayes). Their first play was their best – *The Front Page* – a comedy based on their own experiences as Chicago journalists.

The Chicago writer – the Chicago writer's Chicago writer – was James T Farrell, known best for his novels about lower-middle-class Irish Catholic life on the South Side of the city. They were written in the tradition of naturalism, combined with a modification of the stream-of-consciousness technique and an almost sociological objectivity. Poverty, religious bigotry and narrowness, economic inequality, individual frustration, sordidness, vice and the destructive influence of the environment were emphasized, with contemporary references appropriate to the 1920s

Above: A woodcut impression of Theodore Dreiser in his study by Wharton Esherick.

Left: George Ade (1866-1944), the American humorist and playwright.

and 1930s. His most famous work was his *Studs Lonigan Trilogy*, consisting of *Young Lonigan, The Young Manhood of Studs Lonigan* and *Judgment Day*.

Meyer Levin was a journalist and novelist, known for his studies of American-Jewish and proletarian life, especially in Chicago. One of his best books was *The Old Bunch*, a

Right: A 1922 photograph of Sherwood Anderson (1876-1941), novelist and poet.

novel about young people of Jewish parentage growing up in Chicago in the 1920s, which some critics called 'a Jewish *Studs Lonigan.*'

Pulitzer Prize-winning Thornton Wilder was also in Chicago at the time. This novelist and playwright was known for his sophisticated and ironic novels (*The Bridge of San Luis Rey, Woman of Andros, Heaven's My Destination*) and, later, for his successful plays marked by touches of fantasy and experiments in theatrical techniques (*Our Town, The Skin of Our Teeth, The Trumpet Shall Sound*).

Burton Rascoe was a journalist, reviewer and drama critic. While he was literary editor of the *Chicago Tribune*, he discovered James Branch Cabell. Alfred Kreymborg was a playwright, poet and critic – an original creator of great versatility, but more famous for inspiring other Chicago poets.

There was an area around 57th Street near the old Midway Plaisance, close to the University of Chicago, where a group of fledgling authors formed around Robert Herrick, who had been an associate of William Vaughn Moody, the poet and playwright, before the latter's death. Herrick, a novelist and teacher, felt that Chicago was 'the characteristic American metropolis,' and wanted his novels to contribute to an understanding of modern American life. He was a writer of careful prose and a pioneer realist.

Later, this literary torch would be passed on to other Chicago writers – Nelson Algren (whose *Man with the Golden Arm* and *A Walk on the Wild Side* were to shock the nation), Frank London Brown (whose *Trumbull Park* was the first novel to describe from personal experience what can happen when a

artists and writers lived in their studios. Until about 1924, Towertown was the geographical center of what was perhaps the most vital literary and artistic upsurge in the history of the country. In those years, corn-fed hopefuls from all over the Midwest flowed into the free-and-easy Bohemia that was Chicago. They read their poems to Harriet Monroe at her place at 543 Cass Street. Monroe was a Chicago poet and editor, chiefly known for establishing (in 1912) and editing (until the time of her death in 1936) *Poetry: A Magazine of Verse*, which exercised great influence on American poetry, being open to every sort of experimental work. Some of the writers came to town in hopes of working in the city room of the *Chicago Daily News* with Carl Sandburg and Ben Hecht.

For all of these aspirants, Towertown was perfect. The writers and artists had, to their north, the palaces of the Gold Coast residential area. To their south were the slums of Little Hell, with its good, cheap spaghetti parlors. Towertown was bounded by North Avenue, the main artery of the old German area, on the south by the Chicago River. In the middle of Towertown was the Rialto of North Clark Street, with its saloons, night clubs, gambling joints and brothels. The rent was low, the Loop was within walking distance and the beach was nearby at the foot of Oak Street. And Ireland's, one of the world's best seafood restaurants, was on North Clark Street. What else could an intellectual possibly desire?

But as Prohibition became more and more of a problem, Towertown became the haunt of the Chicago underworld, too. Mobster Dion O'Banion hung out there. He had become famous as a singing waiter at

Above: Upton Sinclair (1878-1968) and his son in a photograph taken when *The Jungle*, Sinclair's exposé of corrupt conditions in Chicago's Union Stock Yards, was published.

Opposite bottom: American poet Vachel Lindsay (1879-1931) left an impressive body of work on native subjects and strove to create a love of poetry in his audiences.

Far right: The American novelist Edna Ferber (1885-1968) in 1920, four years before the publication of *So Big.*

black man moves into a white and hostile Chicago neighborhood) and Saul Bellow (who won the Nobel Prize for Literature in 1976).

As far as literature was concerned, those were truly the Glamour Years in Chicago. Theodore Dreiser had said, 'Chicago was so young, so blithe, so new that just to be a part of it made me crazy with life.' And from far-off Baltimore, H L Mencken sent word that: 'Out in Chicago, the only genuinely civilized city in the New World, they take the fine arts seriously and get into such frets and excitements about them as are raised nowhere else save by baseball, murder, political treachery, foreign wars and romantic loves ... almost one fancies the world bumped by a flying asteroid, and the Chicago River suddenly turned into the Seine.'

In a radius of about a quarter-mile around the Water Tower on North Michigan Avenue was an area known as Towertown, where

Above: The funeral of gangster Hymie Weiss, who was killed in Towertown.

Right: Thornton Wilder (1897-1975) just after he received the Pulitzer Prize for *The Skin Of Our Teeth* in 1942.

McGovern's Liberty Cabaret on North Clark Street before blossoming into a prince of gangdom. 'Yellow Kid' Weil was also a habitué.

Hymie Weiss was machine-gunned down at the corner of State and Superior one autumn afternoon. Towertown had become the site of several gangland killings, and the corner of Oak and Milton Streets in Little Hell was rechristened 'Death Corner.'

Ernest Hemingway, that Oak Park boy, lived in Towertown. Just home from World War I, he was writing about his summers in Charlevoix, Michigan. But even then he went his own way. He lived with an advertising man, Y K Smith, who said of him, 'Hemingway had organized a club in his head, and, having absolute power, he was constantly taking in members and casting out those who failed to meet his standards at a given time.'

Hemingway could be cruel, even in those days. Sherwood Anderson was the established author of *Winesburg, Ohio*, and was working on some poetry – his 'Mid-American Chants.' One of them went:

You know my city –
  factories and cars and roar of machine –
Chicago triumphant;
  horrible, terrible, ugly and brutal.
Can a singer arise and sing in this smoke and live?
Can he keep his throat clear?
Can his courage survive?

Anderson took an interest in Hemingway, and helped him when he could. A few years later, Hemingway repaid him for his interest,

Above: A caricature of humorist Ring Lardner (1885-1933), best known for his engaging baseball stories.

Right: Charles MacArthur (left) and Ben Hecht, who wrote the play *The Front Page*, about life in a Chicago newsroom.

Right: Floyd Dell, the editor and playwright, who did much of his early work in Chicago.

kindness and advice by publishing a savage burlesque of Anderson's work.

Another Chicago writer of the time was beginning to be noticed. He was Ring Lardner, and he followed in George Ade's tradition by writing in natural speech. Lardner was traveling with the Chicago White Sox baseball team when he developed the idea of Jake Keefe, a ballplayer of overwhelming ignorance and vanity, and began to write fiction about professional baseball.

John O'Hara moved to Chicago in 1927, but couldn't get a job, even a menial one. He later recalled Chicago as a very cold place to be without an overcoat. He once said, 'In Chicago I never had any hope. It was not my town. I was too much of an Easterner for it.' But he did use his Chicago memories when he wrote his classic *Pal Joey*.

In 1923 Ben Hecht and Maxwell Boden-

Above: Richard Wright (right), the Chicago novelist, with Count Basie at a recording session in which Basie had made a record of music by Clinton R Brewer, a convict who had been in prison for the past nine years – 24 November 1940, the year that Wright's *Native Son* was published.

Opposite: Ernest Hemingway (1899-1961), the novelist, with his second wife, Pauline, in 1934. They had just returned from a visit to Africa.

Far right: A caricature of Ring Lardner that appeared in his humorous autobiography *The Story of a Wonder Man.*

new tar-smelling subdivisions. Szukalski thrusts his walking stick into the eye-sockets of La Salle Street, Hecht explodes an epithet under the Old Ladies' Home. Beating his bosom, Anderson sinks to his baggy knees gurbling mystically to God. The cubistical Bodenheim ululates on the horizon. Ehu! Ehu! The Pleiocene fogs are drifting.

So much for Chicago. But how about New York? In the same issue, calling New York the 'National Cemetery of Arts and Letters,' Hecht wrote:

The thing that vaguely depresses us about New York is its long ears. The magazines devoted to the Higher Culture – *The Nation, The Dial, The Freeman, The New Republic, The Broom*, and alas, *The Little Review* – stand on the rack of our favorite bookstores and, occasionally, we read them. They depress us. They have long ears. They seem to be suffering from the lack of a good drink or a good physic. They are continually talking about Art as if it were their dead grandmother.

Hecht and Bodenheim had fun reviewing each other's work. Bodenheim called Hecht's *1001 Afternoons in Chicago* 'the vivid etchings of a disillusioned mind, the product of the petty complex of an anti-social American.' Hecht said of Bodenheim's *Blackguard* 'as definite an experience as inhaling a quart of chlorine gas.' At the time, George Groz was doing some drawings for the paper.

But in two years the fun was over and Hecht, Bodenheim and Groz had departed for the 'National Cemetery of the Arts.' One after another, they drifted away – Carl Sandburg, Alfred Kreymbourg, Ernest Hemingway, Ring Lardner, Floyd Dell, Sherwood Anderson, Theodore Dreiser, Burton Rascoe. Most of these greats had arrived in Chicago riding the rods, but they departed in Pullman roomettes.

heim launched the *Chicago Literary Times*. It was published in newspaper format and the price was ten cents a copy. Its philosophy was based on Goethe's statement, 'Praise for another is depreciation of oneself.' Little praise for anybody or anything could be found in the publication.

In the first issue, on 1 March 1923, could be found:

Chicago, the jazz baby – the reeking, cinder-ridden joyous Baptist stronghold: Chicago, the chewing gum center of the world, the bleating, slant-headed rendezvous of half-witted newspapers, sociopaths and pants makers – in the name of the seven Holy and Imperishable Arts, Chicago salutes you.

Civilization overtakes us. The Philoolulu bird lies on its back with its feet in the air – extinct. The Muses, coughing and spitting, reach their arms blindly toward the steel mills and the stockyards.

The cognoscenti pull the flypaper out of their ears. Sandburg's tom-tom sounds through the

Ring Lardner, as pictured in his autobiography "The Story of a Wonder Man"

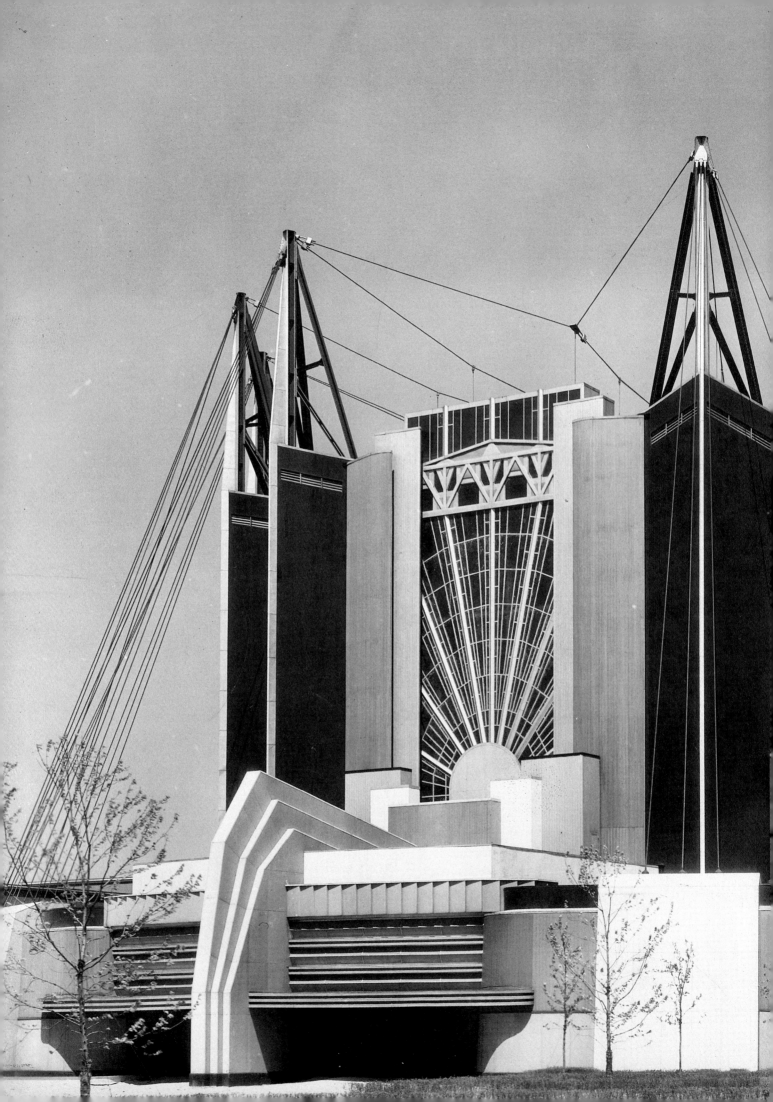

ART AND ARCHITECTURE

Where the fine arts like painting and sculpture are concerned, Chicago has always been, unfortunately, the second city. But there was a glimmering during the Glamour Years.

In the 1920s there was a barn studio on the Midway at the University of Chicago, which the internationally known sculptor Lorado Taft had taken over in 1906. This red-brick barn (later two frame barns were added) was the sculpture capital of the world. Young men and women came there from all over the world to study sculpting under Taft. The ubiquitous Taft could also be found teaching at the Art Institute and at the Fine Arts Building at Van Buren Street and Michigan Avenue.

Beginning in 1935, the center of Chicago's art world was Riccardo's, a restaurant at the lower end of Rush Street. Historically, Chicagoans bought a lot of art works, but they usually went to New York to do it, resulting in a dearth of galleries in the Windy City and the fact that restaurants often attempted to fill that void. Richard 'Ric' Riccardo was a graduate of the WPA Art Project in Chicago, and when he decided to open his new Italian restaurant, he hung the walls with his own paintings.

Some of them were bought by his customers, and Riccardo began to display the work of a different artist each month; finally, he had a monthly exhibition. A lot of this work sold, and artists began to frequent the restaurant. Ric enlarged the bar, and with six other Chicago painters, executed a series of murals. These six friends of Riccardo's went on to become famous. They were: Aaron Bohrod, the two Albright Brothers, Rudolph Weisen-

born, William Schwartz, Vincent D'Agostino, plus, of course, Ric himself.

In the area of architecture, however, Chicago was the pre-eminent city of the world. It was the birthplace of the modern skyscraper and the modern drawbridge. Even though it was a city of neat brick and wood cottages and bulky stone mansions, it produced the geniuses of the Chicago School of Architecture – Louis Sullivan, Daniel Burnham, Dankmar Adler, to name but three, whose innovative tradition was carried on by Frank Lloyd Wright and Ludwig Mies van der Rohe.

Skyscrapers are not new. The first, arguably, was completed in 1885: Chicago's 10-story Home Insurance Building. A physical disaster – the Great Fire – cleared the ground for Chicago's pioneering experiments with tall buildings. The fire left Chicago with a lot of empty lots and a readiness to rely on building materials other than wood. Structural steel – and elevators – made possible America's high-density cities.

Louis Sullivan was the prophet of modern architecture, and out of his Chicago School came many of the world's landmark buildings – those structures that revolutionized architecture the world over. During the Glamour Years, the newer symbols of Chicago carried on the innovation begun by Sullivan, adding to the city's reputation as a place with unparalleled structural beauty, variety, vitality, interest and drama.

It was Sullivan, however, who was responsible for all this. He and his followers, who shared his dream of architecture as formed space, built the city. No matter how great a

Previous pages: The Travel and Transport Building with its sky-hung dome at the 1933 Century of Progress Exhibition in Chicago. At the time it comprised the largest unobstructed area to be enclosed beneath a roof. The roof was formed of metal plates suspended by steel cables hung from a circle of 12 steel towers and anchored by huge slabs of concrete. The dome was 125 feet high and 200 feet across, without a single arch, pillar, beam or other support to break its expanse.

Below right: Louis Henry Sullivan (1856-1924), the architectural genius of Chicago.

Below: Lorado Taft (in smock), the Chicago sculptor, in his studio with some of his students.

Above: The Auditorium ·
Hotel – one of Louis
Sullivan's masterpieces.

Right: The main lobby of the
Auditorium Hotel.

Dining Room. Edgewater Beach Hotel. Chicago.

city is, and however abundant men, money, land and people may be, great architecture cannot be produced without the vision, imagination and genius of an artist.

But why was Chicago unique? She was not unique because she gave great architects the opportunity to rebuild a city destroyed by fire. Boston and San Francisco had also suffered great fires. And it wasn't because of the tremendously rapid increase in size and population, for New York, in common with many other American cities, grew just as rapidly. Chicago is unique in that she alone, from 1875 on, turned to great architects for her city plan and for her buildings.

Great Chicago buildings are a humane expression of a new way of life. They are humane because the architects of the Chicago School, from the first generation of the 1870s and 1880s to the present, have followed the teachings of the master, Louis Sullivan, who said, 'With me, architecture is not an art, but a religion, and that religion but a part of democracy.' In that spirit, Chicago's best buildings and communities were designed. The love of the common man has been the glory of Chicago.

But one of the first buildings to be opened after the end of World War I had nothing to do with the common man. It was an apartment house at 1550 North State Parkway, designed by Benjamin Marshall. Opened in 1918, it was 12 stories high and overlooked the southern reaches of Lincoln Park. The kitchen and pantry sinks were made of German silver. Each of the full-floor apartments had five *chambres de domestique* (the plans were written in French). Two stairways rose in the central well, an *escalier de service* and an *escalier principal*. The rent was $8400 per year, at a time when the *Chicago Tribune*'s daily editions went for two cents a copy and the streetcar fare was seven cents for an adult. Each apartment had a *grand salon* and a *petit salon*, an *orangerie* and a circular room at each end of the building where the towers were. The main bedroom had two dressing rooms 'so that a valet can enter the gentleman's dressing room without passing through the bedchamber.' Other extras included a *caveau de vin*, a garbage chute in each kitchen directly connected to the basement incinerators and a stove with three broilers – two gas and one charcoal – 'so that steaks and fish need never be prepared on the same broiler.'

The architectural firm of Benjamin Howard Marshall and Charles Eli Fox designed the Drake Hotel, which opened on North Michigan Avenue in 1920. It contained the kind of baronial grandeur that could not be duplicated today. The Drake had its Silver Forest Room, used for dining and dancing – a vast room running the whole length of the $8,500,000 hotel's north side.

The Field Museum of Natural History in Grant Park was opened in 1920 – the world's largest natural-history museum.

In 1921 the Wrigley Building was completed – that gleaming terra-cotta skyscraper ornamented with bits and pieces of Renaissance design. Its tower held a four-faced clock two stories high. Not everyone was happy about this Spanish-influenced building. Indeed, Louis Sullivan said that the designers – Graham, Anderson, Probst and White – had crowned the tower with a monstrous spider. An annex was almost immediately begun, and, when it was finished in 1924, there was a bridge connection at the third floor between the annex and the main building.

St Thomas the Apostle Church, at 5472 South Kimbark Avenue, was completed in 1922. It was designed by Barry Byrne, a disciple of Frank Lloyd Wright.

Several landmark buildings were completed in 1923. Among them were the Chicago Temple Building, with its Greek Revival Style; the Centennial Illinois National Bank and Trust Company Building at 213 South La Salle; and the London Guaranty and Acci-

Opposite top: The elaborate dining room of the Edgewater Beach Hotel on Sheridan Road, on the shores of Lake Michigan.

Opposite bottom: The luxury apartment house at 1550 North State Parkway, which opened in 1918.

Below: The Potter Palmer home on Lake Shore Drive, on Chicago's Near North Side.

114

Left: A view from the lower level of the Michigan Avenue Bridge. In the background, left to right: the Wrigley Building, the Medinah Athletic Club and Tribune Tower.

Opposite top: The Avenue of Palms in the Drake Hotel on North Michigan Avenue.

Below: A 1922 photograph of the Field Museum of Natural History (often called the Rosenwald Museum after its benefactor) in Jackson Park.

dent Company Building at 360 North Michigan Avenue.

In 1923 the *Chicago Tribune* announced an international design competition for its new home at 435 North Michigan Avenue. The $10,000 prize attracted designs from all over the world. But something went wrong. The judges gave first place to a striking modern skyscraper designed by Eliel Saarinen of Finland, but the paper's management reversed the decision and the winner was a 36-story design by the New York firm of Raymond Hood and John Meade Howells. The *Chicago Tribune* Tower was to be a Gothic tower with flying buttresses and niches for statues. Saarinen came in second.

Louis Sullivan was aghast, saying, 'It is an imaginary structure – not imaginative.' This was in keeping with the way he had always thought. He was the one who had said, 'When we know and feel that Nature is our friend, not our implacable enemy ... then it may be proclaimed that we are on the high-road to a natural and satisfying art, an architecture that will soon become a fine art in the true, the best sense of the word, an art that will live because it will be of the people, for the people, and by

Previous pages: A photograph of Soldier Field taken from the top of the Field Museum. It is 27 November 1926, and 100,000 people are on hand to watch the kickoff of the Army-Navy football game.

Left: The Grand Dining Room in the Palmer House Hotel.

Opposite: The Straus Building, a Chicago landmark. A W Straus of S W Straus & Company, the owner, offered the building as the site for the proposed Lindbergh Beacon in 1928.

Below: Even the barber shop in the new Palmer House Hotel was magnificent.

the people.' Despite Sullivan's eloquent opposition, the Gothic Revival Tribune Tower was finally completed in 1925.

The Straus Building, at the corner of Jackson Boulevard and Michigan Avenue at 300 South Michigan, was completed in 1924. Its claim to fame was that it was topped with a motif of the Mausoleum of Halicarnassus. Also finished in 1924 was Soldier Field, that massive outdoor arena in Grant Park with room for 101,000 spectators.

In 1925 the old Palmer House Hotel was destroyed to make room for the new Palmer House at State and Monroe Streets. The new hotel was spectacular, but it lacked the Old World charm of its predecessor, which had cost $2,500,000 and featured 34 different kinds of marble inside, a 25-foot-high rotunda, and Egyptian parlor and furnishings imported from France and Italy. Six hundred tons of Belgian iron had been used in its construction. The grand dining room measured 64 by 76 feet and had Corinthian columns, a marble floor and frescoes painted by Italian artists. The dining room featured Scottish damask linen. The new hotel was fine, but Chicago missed the old one.

Actually, some people who cared were becoming worried by all this new construction, which sometimes tore down the old and built the new just because it was new. The prominent architect Frank Lloyd Wright said to reporters in 1925: 'The automobile is going to ruin this city. Michigan Avenue isn't a boulevard, it's a race track! This is a dreadful way to live. You'll be strangled by traffic.'

120

Left: Even in the early 1930s, parking near the Loop was a problem. Here is the parking lot opposite the Illinois Central tracks. In the background, left to right: the Pure Oil Tower, the Mather Tower, the 333 North Michigan Avenue Building and the Wrigley Building.

Opposite top left: A view of downtown Chicago from the Near North Side. Left to right: the Carbide, London Guaranty, Mather and 333 North Michigan Avenue buildings.

Opposite top right: The magnificent Tivoli Theater, at 63rd Street and Cottage Grove Avenue, in 1927.

Below: The Pennsylvania Railroad Train Concourse in the new Union Station.

A reporter asked him, 'What should we do about it?' Wright replied, 'Take a gigantice knife and sweep it over the Loop, cutting off every building at the seventh floor. If you cut down those horrible buildings, you'll have no traffic jams. You'll have trees again. You'll have some joy in the life of this city. After all, this is the job of the architect – to give the world a little joy.'

The architectural highlight of 1927 might well have been the dedication of the Buckingham Memorial Fountain. Located near the lake in Grant Park, it was 280 feet in diameter and featured ever-changing illumination. But there were also important buildings that opened that year. The huge new Union Station Building was completed, as was the 27-story Stevens Hotel (now the Conrad Hilton), which immediately became the largest hotel in the world with its 2600 rooms. Also completed in 1927 was the Lincoln Tower on Wacker Drive, a Gothic Revival building, and the 333 North Michigan Avenue Building – the first Art Deco building in Chicago.

The Rockefeller Memorial Chapel opened on the campus of the University of Chicago at 59th Street and Woodlawn Avenue. It was dedicated to John D Rockefeller Sr, who had given the university so much money that some wags on campus claimed that the university's Alma Mater hymn should be changed to 'Praise John From Whom Oil Blessings Flow.' The Medinah Club, housing the Medinah Lodge of the Shriners, was completed in 1928 and is now a wing of the Hotel Continental.

The Palmolive Building, at the corner of Michigan Avenue and Walton Street, opened its 36 stories in 1929. The Art Deco office building was topped by the Lindbergh Beacon – named for Colonel Charles A Lindbergh – and the light was dedicated on the night of 27 August 1930, when President Herbert Hoover pushed a button in Washington and turned on the two-billion-candle-power beacon in Chicago. The Palmolive Building is now the Playboy Magazine Building.

Also completed in 1929 was Samuel Insull's baby – the huge Civic Opera House on Wacker Drive that covered an entire city block. Insull had taken over the Chicago Opera Company when its chief patron, Harold McCormick, had run out of money. He took the operation from the Adler and Sullivan Auditorium Theater building and moved it to its new 45-story home.

The Carbon and Carbide Building at Michigan Avenue and South Water Street was another 1929 addition. It featured a black Art Deco design with gold trim. That same year the John G Shedd Aquarium opened in Grant Park, at Lake Shore Drive and Roosevelt Road.

While all this construction of office buildings, hotels, museums, fountains and opera houses was going on, Chicago was also concentrating on another type of structure that it would call its own – the gaudy, ornate temples of entertainment. Cornelius and George Rapp were the two architects who made Chicago the center of opulent, but not vulgar, movie houses.

George Rapp once said, 'Watch the eyes of a child as it enters the portals of our great

PATTERSONS
RESTAURANT
900 RUSH ST.

theaters and treads the pathway into fairy-land. Watch the bright light in the eyes of the shopgirl who hurries noiselessly over carpets and sighs with satisfaction as she walks amid furnishings that once delighted the hearts of queens. See the toil-worn father whose dreams have never come true, and look inside his heart as he finds strength and rest within the theater. There you have the answer to why motion picture theaters are so palatial.'

And palatial they were. The Rapps designed, as one of their assignments, the Tivoli Theater, a neighborhood theater on the South Side of Chicago on Cottage Grove Avenue. It had a lobby made of solid marble and modeled after the chapel that Jules Hardouin Mansard had built for Louis XIV at Versailles. When it opened in 1921, the Chicago favorite, Jesse Crawford, was at the organ.

The Rapp's Norshore Theater on West Howard Street, the northern boundary between Chicago and Evanston, opened in 1926 to serve the affluent North Side. It was one of the finest movie theaters ever built. The outer lobby was crowned by crystal chandeliers suspended from a ceiling decorated with Pompeiian motifs. The upper lobby contained gilded bronze, porcelain and fine French antiques. The interior, with its 3000 seats, was of a restrained, yet sumptuous decor – a sort of Louis XVI effect – that reminded theatergoers, if they had ever been there, of the palaces of Paris and St Petersburg.

Above: The Norshore Theater on Howard Street, one of the North Side's most lavish picture palaces, was demolished in the late 1960s.

Opposite top: An interior view of the Moorish-style decor of the Aragon Ballroom, one of Chicago's plushest dance halls — at 1106 West Lawrence Avenue.

Opposite bottom: Another opulent movie house was the Paradise Theater on Crawford Avenue near Washington – 1929.

Previous pages: Chicago by night – a view looking south from the Near North Side.

The Rapps also planned the Oriental Theater on State and Randolph Streets. It opened in 1926, and to walk into the lobby was like taking a trip to the Far East.

John Eberson, Chicago's master of the atmospheric stars-and-clouds effect on the ceiling, designed the Paradise Theater on Crawford Avenue near Washington Boulevard. It opened in 1929.

Along with the movie theaters, Chicago went in for other lavish places of entertainment. The Chez Paree night club at Fairbanks Court and Ontario Street was the supreme Art Deco night club. And when the $1,500,000 Trianon Ballroom opened in 1922, it was one of America's most luxurious dance halls. Paul Whiteman and his Orchestra played at the opening, and the grand march was led by General John J Pershing.

Even after the Stock Market Crash, construction went on, at least of those buildings that had been financed before the crash. The Merchandise Mart at Wells Street and the Chicago River was opened in 1930, with more square footage than any other building in the world until the Pentagon opened in Washington, DC. The Chicago Club Building, a modified, but authentic, version of an Early Renaissance Italian palazzo, was built at the southwest corner of Michigan Avenue and Van Buren Street – on the site of the first Chicago Art Institute – in 1930. Another 1930 addition was the Art Deco Board of Trade, with its statue of Ceres at its summit.

The Field Building, also an Art Deco structure, went up in 1934 on the northeast corner of La Salle and Adams Streets – the site of the first skyscraper, the Home Insurance Building, with its independent metallic structure.

In 1933 Chicago showed its confidence by putting on a World's Fair, which was a celebration of architecture. It was called A Century of Progress, and it was a good show, although it sometimes seemed that Sally Rand was stealing the scene from the architecture with her fan dances.

The World's Fair marked the debut of Rand, who was born Helen Beck in 1904 in the Ozark Mountains. She claimed that she took her surname when she happened to glance at a handy Rand McNally Atlas.

She left home at the age of 13 to become a cigarette girl in a Kansas City night club, and later won bit parts in movies and vaudeville shows. Stranded in Depression-era Chicago when the play in which she was performing folded, she mysteriously splurged a week's salary on a white horse and a trailer. The mystery was solved on the Exposition's opening night, when Rand appeared masquerading as Lady Godiva. Her picture made every newspaper in town, and she quickly received a job at the World's Fair Streets of Paris concession.

Wearing only ostrich feathers held discreetly in front of her, Rand performed her sensuously slow fan dance to Claude

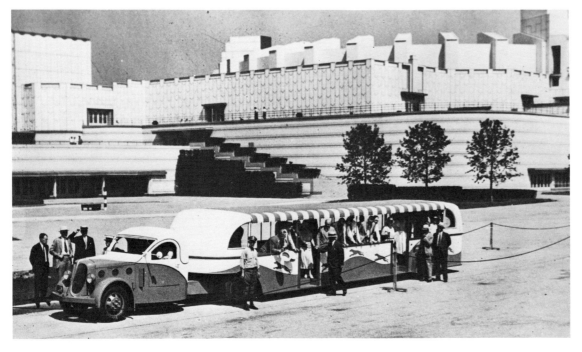

Left: One of the semi-trailer buses that the Greyhound Bus Company used to carry people around at the Chicago World's Fair – A Century of Progress. They were 40 feet long and could carry 90 passengers.

Opposite top: A view of the Chicago World's Fair of 1933-34, looking north from 29th Street. The Hall of Religion is in the foreground.

Opposite bottom: An aerial view of the World's Fair, looking north. The Travel and Transport Building is in the foreground. Behind it are the classically beautiful Chrysler, General Motors and Ford buildings.

Below left: The sensation of Chicago World's Fair was Sally Rand and her renowned fan dance.

Debussy's *Clair de Lune*. Her act alone pulled in enough money to guarantee the financial success of the entire fair. She continued to present the same act at fairs and carnivals for the next 30 years. It was Sally Rand who said, 'They planned this fair to bring business to Chicago, into the Loop. But you could have fired a cannon down State Street and hit nobody, because everybody was out at the Fair, sleeping in their Fords.'

The World's Fair was built in the newly created Burnham Park, on a neck of land near Grant Park that had been filled in, making a harbor and land for the new downtown airport, Meigs Field. Even General Italo Balbo's armada of Italian airplanes flew to the fair (Chicago named Balbo Drive after him). It was so successful that it was held over for another year – ending in the fall of 1934.

A Century of Progress included the Hall of Science, which featured an exhibit on atomic energy – something unheard of at the time. It also had a Sky Ride – a terrifying trip high over the whole fair. The Travel and Transportation Building had a modern suspended roof. The Owens Illinois House started the 1930s fad for glass-block construction.

In addition to this boldly modern architecture, the fair had sculpture by such modernists as Lee Lawrie, Gaston Lachaise, Leo Friedlander, Louise Lentz Woodruff and Carl Milles. Famous works of art were imported for the occasion, too. One of them was *Arrangement in Grey and Black: Portrait of the Artist's Mother* (commonly called *Whistler's Mother*), painted by James Abbot McNeil Whistler, the grandson of the army officer who had built Fort Dearborn. One of the guards at the painting exposition said that he understood the painting was of Hitler's mother.

STAGE AND RADIO

In the early 1920s, Chicagoans could go to Maurice Browne and Ellen Van Falkenberg's Theater in the Fine Arts Building to see plays by Henrik Ibsen and Sir Arthur Wing Pinero. They could go to Jules Goldman's Theater on Cottage Grove Avenue and see one-act plays by Ben Hecht and Kenneth Sawyer Goodman. (Goodman had been killed in World War I, and the Goodman Theater at the Chicago Art Institute was dedicated to his memory.) They could go to a little theater on North Avenue to hear Carl Sandburg read his poems and play his guitar. They could have seen Ben Hecht and Sherwood Anderson's play *Benvenuto Cellini* in several different theaters. They could have discovered Paul Muni when he was an unknown, performing in the theater at Hull House. One of the favorite actors to appear in Chicago was Walker Whiteside – conceded to be one of the finest Shakespearian actors of all time – who never appeared east of Cleveland.

Apart from all this, the theater in Chicago at the time was not a driving force. The houses were always full in the Loop, but the audiences generally had come to see the 'Chicago Company' or the 'National Company' of a play or musical that had opened in New York. Still, actors found Chicago audiences sophisticated and, in general, a tough nut to crack.

Ashton Stevens was the dean of Chicago critics at that time; he worked for William

Randolph Hearst's *Chicago Examiner*. He was known for his feud with Richard Mansfield, the famous actor. He once asked Mansfield if he intended to include George Bernard Shaw's *Arms and the Man* in his repertory. 'If I did,' Mansfield said, 'I'm afraid you wouldn't understand it.' 'Oh,' retorted Stevens, 'I had hoped your diction had improved.'

Stevens was a truly witty man. Once, asked by a theater manager if his seat was satisfactory, he answered 'No, I can not only see, but I can hear every word.'

A gangster was shot as he was leaving a theater one opening night, and Stevens began his review of the play with 'They shot the wrong man.' His mantle of wit and vitriol was later taken over by Claudia Cassidy of the *Chicago Tribune*.

In 1923 the ubiquitous and peripatetic *Blossom Time* was playing at the New Apollo Theater on Randolph Street. It then moved to the Great Northern Theater on Jackson Boulevard, because the cast had been complaining about a tribe of rats that had eaten their makeup sticks and eyebrow pencils. Accommodations in Chicago theaters were not always first-rate.

The theaters in the Loop were not the only places where big-time theater could be seen. There were also 'Satellite Loops,' where actors could work in the big theaters – along Wilson Avenue and Sheridan Road on the North Side; along Milwaukee Avenue and Ashland Avenue on the West Side; around Cottage Grove Avenue and 63rd Street on the South Side.

Radio in the United States got off to a fast start. The first radio station was opened in 1920; almost immediately, it was broadcasting election returns of the Warren G

Previous pages: Freeman Gosden and Charles Correll as 'Amos 'n' Andy,' the extremely popular radio show that had started out as 'Sam 'n' Henry' on WGN Radio in Chicago in 1925.

Below right: The Blackstone Theatre at 60 East Balbo Drive in 1927 – the home of many hit plays over the years.

Below: Carl Sandburg, the poet, in 1930. Sandburg could often be seen and heard playing his guitar and singing folk songs in tiny neighborhood Chicago theaters.

Harding–James M Cox race for the presidency. When Jack Dempsey defeated the French fighter Georges Carpentier, to retain his Heavyweight Boxing Championship of the World at Boyle's Thirty Acres in New Jersey (July 1921), the description of the fight went out over phone lines to 80 stations throughout the country. The stations put it on the air, and America followed it blow by blow. By the winter of 1921–2, radio was truly a national toy, with stations to be found all over the land.

Radio kept growing, and in 1927 the Federal Government had to straighten out the competition by alloting specific wave lengths to stations. That year, America was listening to 'Roxy and His Gang,' 'The Happiness Boys' and 'The A & P Gypsies.' In 1929, one could hear 'The Fada Symphony Orchestra Show,' 'The Pure Oil Band,' 'Paul Whiteman's Old Gold Orchestra Hour,' 'The Freed Orchestradians' and 'The Rudy Vallee Show.' Even though a radio set might cost as much as $135, Americans had bought 12 million of them.

It was in the 1930s that radio came into full flower, and what a variety of programs there were. Jack Benny, Rudy Vallee, Fred Allen, George Burns and Gracie Allen, Bing Crosby and Edgar Bergen and Charlie McCarthy were entertaining millions. The Lone Ranger was so popular that at one time three different episodes were broadcast each week.

And Chicago was a leader in radio.

The original reason that Chicago stepped to the fore in early radio was that New York radio stuck with plays written for the stage and Hollywood was wedded to the screen script. Chicago, however, had always been an innovator, and experimentation was the order of the day. Thus a new art form was invented

in the Windy City – the dramatic play written for radio. Radio drama as we know it actually began in studios in the Merchandise Mart in the middle 1930s. The program was 'First Nighter,' a weekly half-hour drama supposedly set in 'a small theater off Times Square.' It would begin with the hubbub of

Above: The Palace Theater, on vaudeville's Orpheum Circuit, was in the Bismarck Hotel.

Below: Vanity Fair showgirls taking a dip in Buckingham Fountain in Grant Park after a rehearsal.

Above: A combination lamp and radio of 1926. The speaker was located in the lampshade.

Right: Vivienne Osborne was 'Miss Radio of 1928' at the Chicago Radio Show.

first break in Chicago soap operas were Mercedes McCambridge, Joan Blaine, Ann Seymour, Betty Lou Gerson and Harold Peary (who went on to play Gildersleeve on the 'Fibber McGee and Molly' show).

Arch Oboler, a master of the macabre and the Rod Serling of the 1930s, did his best writing in Chicago. His 'Lights Out' weekly dramas scared everyone in the country.

WGN was one of the Chicago independent stations – without a network affiliation. It was owned by the *Chicago Tribune*, whose owner, Colonel Robert R McCormick, had modestly picked out the call letters, which stood for World's Greatest Newspaper. Beginning in 1925, WGN aired a modest quarter-hour comedy series called 'Sam 'n' Henry.' Freeman F Gosden and Charles J Correll, two white men, played all the parts in this continued tale of two black men and their friends. The program moved in 1928 to WMAQ, an NBC Blue Network affiliate, then owned by the *Chicago Daily News*, to get national exposure. The *Tribune* claimed that it owned the original title for the show, so the program was re-christened 'Amos 'n' Andy,' and lasted for 20 years on the radio. It has been said that one could walk down the street on a summer evening and follow the show without missing a word, because the sound of the program was coming through every open window on the block.

The show was all about the adventures of the good and faithful Amos, who ran a taxi company, and the shiftless and plotting Andy, who was always trying to earn a fast buck. Of course, it was racist, but it was well written, and such phrases as 'I'se regusted' and 'Check and double check' became part of

the theater, and then an usher would greet the host by saying, 'Step this way, Mr First Nighter.' This program made Don Ameche famous, and Les Tremayne and Barbara Luddy temporarily well known.

Chicago radio writers also invented the soap opera, short fifteen-minute playlets whose plots went on forever. They were broadcast daily from Chicago: it seemed as if there were hundreds of them going out over the Columbia Broadcasting System and National Broadcasting Company stations (at the time NBC consisted of two networks, the Red and the Blue' later the Red Network became the American Broadcasting Company). Notable soaps included 'Stella Dallas,' 'Ma Perkins,' 'Vic and Sade' (a now forgotten, delightfully humorous soap which, in its heyday, was heard four times a day and used two different scripts for the broadcasts), 'Our Gal Sunday,' 'Myrt and Marge,' 'Lorenzo Jones,' 'Helen Trent' and countless others.

Among those radio actors who got their

Americans' vocabularies. It was also insightful at times, as when Amos explained a new insurance policy to Andy: 'The big print give it to you, and the little print take it away.'

Chicagoans could also be treated to 'The Chicago Theater of the Air' every week. This hour-long show featured an abridged operetta, sung by excellent performers, and was broadcast on WGN. It was thoroughly enjoyable, and all one had to pay for the entertainment was to suffer through one of Colonel McCormick's isolationistic speeches between acts.

There were many other local programs to be enjoyed. Norman Ross broadcast 60 minutes of light classical music every morning on his 'Northwestern Hour.' José Bethancourt could be heard playing his marimba, accompanied by his orchestra, on WMAQ's 'Echoes of the Tropics.' (No one knows why the marimba was so big in Chicago, but a hundred-piece marimba band would often play a few numbers at the annual 'Chicagoland Music Festival' in Soldier Field, and everyone wondered where they all came from.) Ralph Ginsburg and his Palmer House Ensemble had a tea dance show.

The informal chat or kaffe-klatsch shows started in Chicago, too. Pat Barnes and East and Dumke were doing this type of broadcasting long before Jack Paar, Johnny Carson and Phil Donahue were out of school.

'Club Matinee' was unique. It was an hour-long show broadcast every day but Sunday – a

mixture of comedy, music and talk. Music lovers in particular would live for the weekly appearance of the Stedgie Prep band, combined with the boys of the Burp County Fireman's Band, who would butcher some old light classic like 'The William Tell Overture' or 'Morning, Noon and Night in Vienna.' This must have been fun for the

Above: Two favorites of Chicago's night life were 'The Incomparable Hildegarde' and band leader Paul Whiteman.

Left: The Rock Island Railroad's *Golden State Limited* left Chicago bound for Los Angeles carrying radio equipment. Along the way it picked up signals from stations in Chicago; Hastings; Nebraska; Kansas City; Davenport; Iowa; Des Moines; Denver; Fort Worth; Dallas and several California cities.

WMAQ orchestra, who worked so hard to play off-key and out of tempo while using their worst techniques.

The master of ceremonies of all this was the pixieish comic Ransom Sherman. Sherman was a small-town boy from Appleton, Wisconsin who had worked in radio for years until he became host of 'Club Matinee' in 1937. When the six-day-a-week chore became too much, he found a crew-cut youngster to take over three of the six weekly programs. This was a lad named Thomas Garrison Morfit. Of course, that name would never do, and WMAQ offered a $50 prize in a 'Rename Morfit' contest. Thus emerged Garry Moore, who became not only a performer, but a student of Sherman's, learning to write and perform comedy.

In July of 1941, with 'Club Matinee' still on the air, Sherman became 'Hap Hazard,' proprietor of Crestfallen Manor, part of the Stop and Flop chain of penurious inns. The program was used that year as the summer replacement for 'Fibber McGee and Molly.' Whatever the format, Sherman was always the unsophisticated 'just plain folks' character who stood a bit apart from the dramatic insanity going on about him. In addition to Moore, a couple of other Sherman discoveries were Jonathan Winters and Fran Allison, who was the female singer on his show long before she teamed up with Burr Tillstrom on 'Kukla, Fran and Ollie' (also a Chicago show).

'Don McNeill's Breakfast Club,' from WENR of the NBC Red Network, was a national institution for years. Everyone knew it was corny and unsophisticated, but there was so much warmth and love and so much comedy and good music on the show that all America listened to it at breakfast time. Walter Blaufuss and the orchestra were

Opposite top: Tris Speaker (right), the legendary baseball player, was the broadcaster covering the home games of the Chicago Cubs and Chicago White Sox on WENR/WLS. Also in the photo are Senator Kaney (left) and Roger Hornsby – 'The Rajah.'

Left: Les Tremayne and Barbara Luddy in 1941. They were the long-lasting stars of the 'First Nighter' radio show originating on WBBM.

Below: The legs belong to Madaline Parker, a chorus girl from the stage musical *The Time, the Place and the Girl.* She is recording a tap dance at the Brunswick Recording Studios in Chicago – 1930.

capable musicians, and The Escorts and Betty were clever in their comic songs and could also harmonize on a ballad. Sam Cowling was an effective second banana to McNeill. Male and female singers came and went. Johnny Desmond got his start on the show, as did, years later, Anita Bryant.

Kids were not neglected in those days, either. There were many kiddie soaps available just before dinner time. 'Jack Armstrong,' 'Captain Midnight,' 'Don Winslow of the Navy' and many more were favorites, but the champion was probably 'Little Orphan Annie.'

Sponsored by Ovaltine, the program was one of the most popular of all time. Actually, most kids hated Ovaltine, but they would nag their mothers to buy it so that they could save the aluminum foil seals for such things as the Little Orphan Annie Decoder Ring. Messages would be read to them in code, which they would decode on the ring. Most often they said such things as 'Annie is in trouble' or 'Eat your vegetables,' but the decoding was the fun of it all. Another premium was the Ovaltine shake-up mug, a garish plastic kiddy cocktail shaker, that, of course, encouraged the purchase of even more Ovaltine.

The show was introduced on radio, following the success of the comic strip, on 6 April 1931, and ran until 1940. Each show opened

with the announcer, Pierre André, introducing the theme song:

> Who's that little chatterbox?
> The one with pretty auburn locks?
>   Who can it be?
> It's Little Orphan Annie.
> She and Sandy make a pair.
> They never seem to have a care.
>   Cute little she,
> It's Little Orphan Annie.
> Bright eyes, cheeks a rosy glow
> There's store of healthiness handy.
> Pint-size, always on the go,
> If you want to know, 'Arf' goes Sandy.
> Always wears a sunny smile,
> Now wouldn't it be worth your while,
>   If you could be
> Like Little Orphan Annie?

Then came the adventure episode.

Another favorite with the moppets was 'Jolly Joe,' an early morning quarter-hour that caught kids as they were getting ready for school. Joe Kelly, with his terrible singing voice, his out-of-tune piano and his warmth and love for kids, fascinated everybody (he was later to be the master of ceremonies and question-asker on 'The Quiz Kids' program). He organized fake dressing races (checking on the children with his magic telescope), pick-up parades (to help the mothers) and saving drives.

Once a week the kids would put their money into their piggy banks to the accompaniment of Jolly Joe singing, to the tune of 'Tramp, Tramp, Tramp the Boys Are Marching':

> When we march up to our bank
> We have Mother and Dad to thank
> For the pennies we are saving day by day.
> And how glad we all should be
> Whether it's only one or three
> In this land we dearly love, so great, so free.

This bit of doggerel fascinated his listeners, as did his theme song:

> Tie a little string around your finger
>   So you'll remember me.
> Anything you can to make me linger
>   In your memory.
> If you all will listen in to Jolly Joe
>   Oh how happy I would be.
> So tie a little string around your finger
>   So you'll remember me.
> Bum! Bum!

The program was presented over station WLS, which was first owned by Sears, Roebuck (the call letters stood for the World's Largest Store) and later by *The Prairie Farmer*, a rural newspaper. WLS and WENR, both of the National Broadcasting Company's Red Network, shared time on the same dial setting. And juvenile fans of Jolly Joe would often stay on to hear the country music programs that followed him on WLS –

Above: Marian and Jim Jordan got their start as 'Fibber McGee and Molly' on Chicago's WMAQ radio.

Right: Fran Allison (a radio singer later to become famous as the Fran of 'Kukla, Fran & Ollie' on television) was a frequent guest of host Don McNeill on 'The Breakfast Club' emanating from WENR, Chicago. She always played 'Aunt Fanny' on the show, giving out home-spun gossip, advice and stories.

Above: Cast and sound men of 'Gang Busters' — another popular Chicago radio show.

Far right: Red Foley, one of the mainstays of Chicago's 'National Barn Dance' radio show from WLS.

Red Foley was born in Blue Lick, Kentucky in 1910, and grew up playing guitar and harmonica. At the age of 17 he won a state-wide singing championship, singing gospel. In 1932 he graduated from Georgetown College in Kentucky, but he was deep into music and joined the 'Barn Dance' immediately after graduation. For a while on the show, he was a member of the Cumberland Ridge Runners with Lulu Belle (who was later to team with Scotty Wiseman as Lulu Belle and Scotty), but he became an audience favorite as a soloist.

In Chicago, Foley absorbed blues and jazz stylings into his traditional country and gospel sound. This brought more character and a broader appeal to his singing. His rich, polished baritone could now appeal to Northern and urban ears as well as his considerable country audience.

George Gobel began his career as a country singer and comic at an earlier age than most country-Western legends. Gobel was born in 1919 in Chicago, and by the age of 13 was a star on the 'Barn Dance.' Billed as 'Little Georgie Gobel' and 'The Little Cowboy,' he was indeed little. Part of his act was calling his tiny ukelele a guitar, pretending to think that he was fooling the audience. His musical talents were real, and he performed country and cowboy songs flawlessly,

Working on 'The National Barn Dance' was like attending a school for comedians, since comics on the show, plus their guests, such as Homer and Jethro, Amos 'n' Andy, Lum and Abner, and Fibber McGee and Molly, were good teachers. Gobel remained with the 'Barn Dance' until World War II, when he was drafted. Later, of course, he became a TV comedy star.

singing by the Maple City Four, Lulu Belle and Skyland Scottie, and others. Thus they got a taste of one of the nation's most popular country and Western radio shows – 'The National Barn Dance' – which was heard on the network, originating from Chicago on WLS, every Saturday night. A lot of stars got their first shot at fame on that program.

Eddie Peabody was on the show for years, and always had a solo or two to play. He was the master of the banjo and his strumming and picking enthralled the audiences.

Zeke Clements was a comedian and singer of eclectic abilities, and performed a variety of musical styles all over the continental United States – he even provided one of the dwarfs' voices in Walt Disney's *Snow White*. Born near Empire, Alabama, Clements showed an early proclivity toward comedy and music. As a boy he hung around the pioneer country radio station WSB; he worked in vaudeville with rural comedians the Weaver Brothers and Elviry; he toured with burlesque shows. On WHO in Des Moines, he teamed with Texas Ruby Owens. Clements joined the WLS 'Barn Dance' in 1928 when it was the nation's leading country radio show, and was an immediate sensation with his earthy comedy and rough singing style.

Above: Gene Autry got his first big break on WLS's 'National Barn Dance'.

Above right: The singing hillbilly comedians, Homer and Jethro, made many appearances on 'The National Barn Dance'.

Opposite: Country and Western singer Patsy Montana was the queen of the cowgirls on 'The National Barn Dance' for many years.

Patsy Montana was born Ruby Blevins in Hot Springs, Arkansas, and grew up admiring the music of Jimmie Rogers and Gene Autry – there being few female singers to follow at the time. She attended the University of Western Louisiana and performed locally on the side, taking her stage surname in honor of Monte Montana, the champion yodeler, when she formed the Montana Cowgirls. She appeared in a few Western films, and then went to visit the Chicago World's Fair in 1933.

There she met a male ensemble called the Prairie Ramblers and joined the group as the lead singer. She and the Ramblers were an act for 15 years, and Patsy was a member of the 'Barn Dance' until well into the 1950s. Patsy Montana and the Prairie Ramblers were an eclectic, good-times ensemble that reflected disparate musical influences: gospel, pop, jazz (they often used sax and clarinet), purple lyrics, Western swing, honky-tonk and even polka rhythms.

Probably the most famous alumnus of the 'National Barn Dance' was Gene Autry. Orvon Gene Autry was born on a tenant farm in Tioga, Texas, in 1907, and was raised in Ravia, Oklahoma. After high school he worked with the Fields Brothers Marvelous Medicine Show and then, more convention-ally, for the St Louis and Frisco Railroad as a telegrapher in Sapulpa, Oklahoma. One night in 1925, he was singing at his station to pass the time and a stranger complimented his voice, advising him to turn professional. That stranger was Will Rogers, and Gene deter-mined that he would make a career in music.

In 1927, after adding yodeling to his style, he cut some records with no success, but was discovered by a recording executive and billed as Oklahoma's Singing Cowboy. It was in 1929 that Gene recorded his own song 'That Silver-Haired Daddy of Mine.' The song became a hit and sold more than five million copies. Autry then became a featured star on the 'Barn Dance' from 1931-4, where he sang his soft yodels and hillbilly songs. While he was in Chicago, Sears, Roebuck (which still owned WLS) marketed thousands of Gene Autry records, guitars and song-books. But Autry signed a film contract in 1934, and the rest is history.

WLS was top-notch in publicising the 'National Barn Dance.' At any given time, there would be a small troupe of performers at schools in Chicago – during the day or the evening – putting on assembly programs, free, of course. Usually an important star like George Gobel would bring some of the supporting performers along. That might be Hotan-Tonka, the supposed Indian chief, or Max Terhune, the cowboy ventriloquist, with his dummy, Skully. Terhune later went to Hollywood and joined the Three Mesquiteers cowboy team. He took Skully along.

POLITICS AND STRIFE

'Chicago,' it has been said, 'did not invent urban political corruption, but the city perfected it into a municipal institution, with a hard-hitting, quid pro quo, punch-in-the-nose style.' In Chicago, politics has always been a spectator sport.

William 'Big Bill' Thompson was the mayor who perhaps personified this municipal corruption. He was elected mayor in 1915 and served two non-consecutive terms before he was thrown out.

Thompson was wealthy and in the beginning had the admiration of his fellows, but he blew it. The thing that defeated him was his lack of common sense, On being sworn into office, his first announcement was that 'Crooks had better move out.' The next thing that Chicagoans knew was that the South Wabash Street restaurant run by 'Big Jim' Colosimo, undoubtedly the Chicago crime boss of the time, was reopened after it had been closed by the previous mayor, Carter Harrison, for failure to obey the closing laws and other overlooked violations.

Thompson would settle a streetcar strike to the cheers of his constituents, then turn around and order taverns to close on Sundays, changing the cheers to boos. He hired thousands of temporary employees to whom he owed favors, often firing Civil Service personnel to make room for them.

After war was declared in 1917, he made speeches opposing the draft and refused to invite important French officials to Chicago during their American tour. So isolationistic was Thompson that he once threatened to punch King George V of England 'in the snoot' if he ever came to Chicago.

Things got so bad that Thompson was expelled from the Rotary Club, and the Illinois Athletic Club removed his picture from their wall. The Bishop of Baltimore suggested that he be shot as a traitor. The Society of Veterans of Foreign Wars hanged him in effigy for allowing a fascist rally to be held. He truly couldn't win. During his two terms in office, prostitution, gambling and bootlegging flourished. Thompson died in 1944, and a *Chicago Daily News* editorial called him 'the most unbelievable man in Chicago history.'

Aiding and abetting Thompson all the way were 'Bathhouse John' Coughlin and Mike 'Hinky Dink' Kenna, the aldermen who ran the 1st Ward for over 40 years. The 1st Ward

Previous pages: Mayor William Hale Thompson (in the fur coat) dedicating two public improvements on 20 December 1930 – the widening of La Salle Street and the opening of the Wabash Avenue Bridge.

Opposite top: A car barn is closed during the elevated and streetcar carmen's strike in 1919.

Right: Eugene V Debs, the labor leader, in 1908.

Far right: Madison Street during the carmen's strike of 1919. Because there was no public transportation, people either walked or shared rides on trucks.

was on the South Side, and its center of corruption was known as The Levee – five solid blocks north of 22nd Street between Clark Street and Wabash Avenue.

Bathhouse John was master of the malaprop. He once told a mayor, 'You won because of the well-known honesty which has caricatured your administration.' He appointed himself Chicago's 'Poet Lariat.' He had once been a masseur in a bathhouse, hence the nickname, but he ended his reign as alderman with a stable of thoroughbreds, a castle in Orlando, Florida, a private zoo and the most expensive male wardrobe in North America: he changed several times a day.

Hinky Dink also made a fortune. He and John were responsible for bartering for votes in their ward, and never failed to deliver the ward at election time. They used intimidation, mayhem, murder, and parades of armies of alcoholic derelicts to vote at the polls, giving them beer slops and the leavings in liquor glasses from the saloons under their control.

Populism was beginning to surface in Chicago in 1919. Speakers at a Socialist mass meeting in the Chicago Coliseum expressed sympathy for the Russian Bolshevist revolutionaries and called for a dictatorship of the proletariat in the United States. An editorial in the *Chicago Daily News* protested that anyone who advocated such a thing 'writes himself down a poor citizen and poor thinker. Such doctrines should be repudiated by the wage earner, as they are sure to be repudiated by every other truly American element of our population that has grasped the meaning of our institutions and our national ideas and principles.' Of course, the average man, Chicagoan or not, then and now, was indifferent to both the Socialists and the editorial writers.

People learned during World War I to strike down the thing that they hated, however, and now it was the time to strike down Bolsheviks. The nation at war had formed the habit of summary action. Labor agitators were a bunch of Bolsheviks, anyway, and it was about time that a man had a chance to make a decent profit in his business. On the other hand, Labor had found that it was no longer unpatriotic to go out on strike.

Meanwhile, people expected the marching of Bolshevik boots and the explosion of Bolshevik bombs. It was an era of lawlessness

and disorderly defense of law and order, of unconstitutional support for the Constitution, of suspicions and civil conflict – a reign of terror. The only justification for all this antagonism was the number of strikes called after World War I by stockyard workers, shoe workers, carpenters, and others. In November of 1919, the total number of workers on strike in the United States was at least two million. But even in 1919, there were only 39,000 Socialists, 10-30,000 members of the Communist Labor Party and 30-60,000 members of the Communist Party. Even if all of them were radical, and most were not, they would comprise only two-tenths of one percent of the adult population of the United States. By 1921 the Red Scare was almost over. It had all been a mistake that would be almost forgotten until the McCarthy Era.

But racial problems were also beginning to surface. What was done to house the black families who had come north to Chicago to work in the war industries? The main area where they lived, called Bronzeville, held 100,000 blacks, who had settled in what had once been residential neighborhoods of the white middle class. This area ran from the University of Chicago through Washington Park and south of the Levee District from 21st to 63rd Streets.

The Polish-American and Bohemian-American businessmen on the South Side resented the presence of blacks in Chicago. They enjoyed their neighborhood life and wanted no changes. One reporter who investigated this situation was Carl Sandburg of the *Chicago Daily News*. On 13 July 1919, he started working on a series about life in Bronzeville. He went there and talked to a white realtor on Wentworth Avenue – one of many interviews he conducted with both whites and blacks. At the time, Wentworth Avenue was one of the boundaries between white and black neighborhoods on the South Side. He asked the realtor about the bomb explosions on the porches of houses rented by blacks in the white neighborhood east of Wentworth Avenue.

The man answered 'Not one cent has been appropriated by our real estate board for bombing or anything like that. But I would say to the Negroes, "We might as well be frank about it. You people are not admitted to our society." Oh, I've done business with them and they've paid. I've never had to foreclose. But, you know, improvements are coming along the Lake Shore, the Illinois Central and all that. We can't have these people coming over here. They hurt our values. I can't say how many have moved in, but there's at least a hundred blocks that are tainted. We are not making any threats, but we do say that something must be done. Of

Below: The corner on Cottage Grove Avenue where the 1919 riots took place – a photo taken on 30 July 1919. Twenty-eight people were killed and more than 500 wounded; 4600 National Guard troops were sent in to restore order.

Above: A Chicago policeman tries to aid an injured black during the race riots of 1919.

Right: Carl Sandburg, the reporter who predicted the race riots, with some of his admirers in 1933.

Following pages: A 1931 Chicago parade featured floats, bands, livestock, boys and girls of the 4-H Club, butchers, sausage makers and employees from every unit of the stockyards, including the 'Farmerettes,' seen here. The reason for the parade was to point out the importance of meat industries and consumption to the city; the message was 'Eat more meat.'

course, if they come in as tenants, we can handle that situation fairly easily. We want to be fair and do what's right.'

Sandburg then interviewed the secretary of a black YMCA, who said, 'The colored people see that if they can't make it in Chicago, it's no use for them to go back South. But there has always been fighting between the Black Belt and the Wentworth Avenue crowd.' Sandburg saw a confrontation coming and warned the people of Chicago in his articles in the *Daily News*.

He knew that the whites were turning on the blacks, who were beginning to feel their independence. Had they not fought in the war the same as whites? Had they not worked in the war industries the same as whites? When it came time to put them into their place again, they were not too willing to have this happen, and the whites began to fear the situation.

The confrontation predicted by Carl Sandburg came at the end of that very month – July 1919. The black and white people who used the 31st Street Beach on the South Side had always kept it segregated – part for white, part for black – by mutual understanding. In the summer of 1919, a 17-year-old black youth

Above: Representative Oscar DePriest, Congressman from the First District of Illinois and the first black to serve in Congress since Reconstruction.

Below: Police advance on strikers against Republic Steel.

For nearly a week, Chicago was in a state of virtual civil war. Blacks were mobbed, beaten, stabbed. Whites were shot by blacks. Fighting gangs took to the streets. After two days of street fighting, in which both whites and blacks were killed, Mayor Thompson, on 30 July, sent the militia into the South Side in taxis and trucks. One militiaman killed a white man with his bayonet when he refused to move on.

The death toll of this violent confrontation was 14 whites and 22 blacks – some shot, some knifed, some trampled with their spines stamped to bits and their chests and faces kicked in. There were 537 people injured and 1000 left homeless. A judge, Robert R Crowe, called for the death penalty for the ruffians who had participated in the five-day explosion, but nothing ever came of it.

Chicago, however, has always been hard to predict. Just nine years later, in 1928, the city elected the first black United States Representative since George Henry White, who had served in the United States Congress during Reconstruction. The name of the Chicago Congressman was Oscar DePriest. At the same time, Robert Sengstacke Abbott, the publisher of the *Chicago Defender*, the black newspaper, was said to be the first black millionaire in the United States.

Big Bill Thompson lost the election in

was swimming off the shore on the black side. The boy, holding on to a railroad tie, went across the invisible line. Stones were thrown at him and a white man swam toward him. This frightened the black man, who let go of the tie, sank, and drowned. The blacks on shore accused the whites of stoning him to death and a fight began, starting a bonfire of racial hatred.

Above: An editorial cartoon featuring Samuel Gompers, who is sitting on lids trying to calm down his American Federation of Labor colleagues.

Below: Dairy farmers in the Chicago area dump milk from one of the non-strikers' trucks during the milk strike of September 1933.

1931, but new mayor Anton 'Tony' Cermak simply brought in another crooked machine. When Cermak was killed in Florida in 1933, he was succeeded by Edward J Kelly, who served from 1933 to 1947 and was described as a watered-down Bill Thompson.

Race problems arose again in Bronzeville in 1931. The Great Depression was the cause of many evictions there, and riots broke out on 3 August. On that day, three rioters had been shot and killed by the police when, according to the *Chicago Tribune*, 'Three thousand Communists, mainly colored, abandoned a parade and started a battle to prevent the legal eviction of a family from quarters at 5016 South Dearborn Street.' Mayor Cermak, who was vacationing on Mackinac Island in Michigan, sent orders for police and city officials to make certain that nothing endangered law and order. The *Tribune* claimed that there had been 'thousands of shock troops of the Reds involved' and that they had been taught to speak to each other in Esperanto. 'The Communist regime, centered at Moscow, has declared war against democratic America and its invasion should be met and defeated.' What nonsense.

One of the gut-wrenching sights of 1932 was a crowd of blacks standing tight-packed in front of a Chicago tenement to prevent the landlord from evicting a neighbor family. The group sang hymns for hour after hour.

On 4 March 1933, Governor Henry Horner of Illinois proclaimed a bank holiday in the state. This was Franklin D Roosevelt's inauguration day. Roosevelt was to call a national bank holiday on the following day – one that would last until 13 March.

One of the worst riots occurred on Memorial Day of 1937, at the South Chicago plant of Republic Steel, whose president was Tom M Girdler. At the time, United States Steel had come to terms with the Steel Workers' Union Organizing Committee, but a group of steel companies, known as 'Little Steel,' held out. This group included Republic Steel, Inland Steel, Bethlehem Steel and the Youngstown Sheet and Tube Corporation.

Anticipating trouble, Youngstown bought eight machine guns, 360 rifles, 190 shotguns, 540 revolvers and 10,000 rounds of ammunition in the spring of 1937, plus 109 gas guns with 3000 cartridges. Republic did more, spending $79,000 for tear gas alone.

On 30 May 1937, Republic strikers from the South Chicago plant were listening to speakers in a meeting hall. The meeting ended and about 300 people started to walk toward the plant entrance, where police were waiting for them. This was not a mob, but an unorganized crowd in which people were walking in twos and threes.

The police fired and 10 people were dead in the first 30 seconds, with 90 wounded. The police then chased the fleeing crowd, knocking down and beating 28 more. They had beaten them so severely that they were hospitalized, along with three of the police who had been pelted by stones.

It turned out that seven of the dead had been shot in the back and three in the side – but none in the front. The strike had failed at Republic, but workers were outraged, which gave impetus to the efforts of John L Lewis's organizers. Four years later the National Labor Relations Board recognized the United States Steel Workers of America.

CRIME AND CORRUPTION

Previous pages: Bodies are carried from the Clark Street garage after the 1929 St Valentine's Day Massacre.

Opposite top: A statue over the door of a brewery closed during Prohibition. The brewery was located on South Michigan Avenue.

Opposite bottom: A view from the corner of 27th Street and the aptly named Brewery Avenue during Prohibition. This had been one of the liveliest business sections of Chicago, with its numerous beer-making establishments.

Below: Members of Chicago's Anti-Saloon League meet to plan their campaign to dry up the whole world following their success with Prohibition in America. They voted to open a concerted drive on Europe, Asia and the British Isles, with Germany and Austria to be the first victims. The plan didn't work.

During World War I, the country was largely dry by state law and local option. When the Eighteenth Amendment to the Constitution was passed, the *New York Tribune* said that it was 'as if a sailing ship on a windless ocean were sweeping ahead, propelled by some invisible force.' By 16 January 1919, 36 states had ratified the amendment; in the end, only Connecticut and Rhode Island did not do so. It seemed as if whiskey and the 'liquor rings' were as hated as the Bolsheviks.

In 1919 the bars were serving mainly Scotch highballs and Bronxes – the latter a horrible concoction of one-half orange juice, one-fourth gin, one-eighth dry vermouth and one-eighth sweet vermouth. But Prohibition was approaching, to begin on 1 July. Even in early 1919, distilling and brewing were against the law, and that made liquor expensive. Usually there were no women at the bar, because women's drinking was rare. There were no such things as cocktail parties – tea parties were more common. The typical reaction from the American male about Prohibition was, 'I'll miss my liquor for a time, but the boys will be better off for living in a world where there is no alcohol.'

The first Prohibition commissioner, John F Kramer, had declared, 'This law will be obeyed in cities, large and small, and in villages, and where it is not obeyed it will be enforced. . . . The law says that liquor to be used as a beverage must not be manufactured.

Not sold, nor given away, not hauled in anything on the surface of the earth or under the sea or in the air.' How wrong he was.

There were problems. The United States had 18,700 miles of coastline – ideal for rumrunning. Druggists could sell alcohol on prescriptions. Near beer (whoever named it that had a poor sense of distance) was legal, but beer had to be brewed to remove the alcohol from near beer. Industrial alcohol was legal. Citizens could buy a legal commercial still for their homes for $500 and produce 50 to 100 gallons of booze per day. Even a one-gallon portable still would go for six or seven dollars.

There were other problems. In 1920 only 1520 men were acting as Prohibition agents. This was raised to a mere 2836 in 1930 – to police a US population of over 123 million. Aid from the Coast Guard, the Customs Service and the Immigration Service was often unenthusiastic. Agents were paid from $40 to $50 per week – hardly a sum to hire a diligent expert, or one who could resist temptation. And the states wouldn't back the agents: by 1927 they were spending less money on professional liquor prohibition than on enforcing their own fish and game laws. Actually, they spent eight times more on fish and game enforcement.

Speakeasies were the rage. The popular drink was a cocktail made from gin; it cost 75 cents for patrons and was free to the police.

Hotels served setups provided by the management. Of course, these were to be consumed providing that they 'were not to be mixed with spiritous liquids.' But nobody, not even the management, paid any attention to that.

Humorists wrote about Prohibition. Franklin 'FPA' Pearce Adams wrote in his 'Conning Tower' column in the *New York Post* in 1931:

Prohibition is an awful flop.
  We like it.
It can't stop what it's meant to stop.
  We like it.
It's left a trail of graft and slime,
It's filled our land with vice and crime,
It didn't prohibit worth a dime.
  Nevertheless we're for it.

The Hoosier commentator, Elmer Davis, said it best. 'The old days when father spent his evenings at Cassidy's Bar with the rest of the boys are gone, and probably gone forever. Cassidy may still be in business at the old stand, and father may still go down there of evenings, but since Prohibition mother goes down with him.'

George Ade missed the Chicago saloons. 'During the nineties all of the alluring vices flaunted themselves in the open. Satan had all of his merchandise in the show-windows. The managers of the prolonged carnival did not kill one another. They co-operated, in the most friendly manner.'

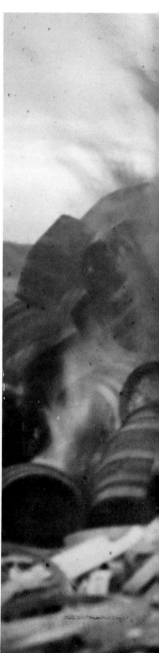

Defiance of the Prohibition law was immediate. And what a change occurred. The hip flask came in. People started to prefer distilled booze to fermented. The saloon became a speakeasy, and the all-male bar catered to both sexes. A large element of the American public had learned to live with impunity on the fruits of lawbreaking, and others enjoyed the criminality. What better place for the revolution to occur than in Chicago?

When Prohibition went into effect, the Chicago gangs were ready to help ease the city's thirst, since they had been well established since the beginning of the Bill Thompson regime. Many of these gangsters had been imported to assist during the newspaper distribution wars earlier in the century between William Randolph Hearsts' *Chicago Examiner* and the *Chicago Tribune*, where they were used to intimidate truck drivers, newsdealers and even newsboys. When the wars were over, many of them stayed in the city. Others were imported to work for people like 'Big Jim' Colosimo, the opera lover and brothel proprietor (and boss of the underworld), whose restaurant was safely within the wide-open 1st Ward, run by aldermen Mike 'Hinky-Dink' Kenna and 'Bathhouse John' Coughlin. It was Colosimo who brought his nephew, Johnny Torrio, from New York to help him out with the problem of Black Hand extortionists in 1909. Torrio fixed things by having a couple of Black Hand mobsters blown away, and stayed on to help his uncle.

During the winter of 1919–20, Colosimo grew tired of his wife, the hard-working Victoria Moresco. He had hired a girl singer,

Dale Winter, to warble at his cafe and fell in love with her. Naturally, Colosimo got fast service in the courts for a divorce in March of 1920, and married Dale three weeks later. They returned from their honeymoon in early May and Big Jim was killed almost immediately, on 11 May. The funeral was held on 15 May, but Chicago's Cardinal Mundelein forbade burial in holy ground and shut the doors of all Roman Catholic churches against services for Colosimo because of his divorce and remarriage.

However, the family found a clergyman, Father Pasquale de Carol, to conduct services in Colosimo's Vernon Avenue mansion. In the funeral procession to Oakwood Cemetery were 1000 members of the 1st Ward Democratic Club, with Coughlin and Kenna in the lead. There was a brass band followed by open carriages crammed with flowers. Three municipal judges followed in a car, an assistant state's attorney in another car, then nine aldermen walked behind that, along with mobsters, including Johnny Torrio. Following them were city employees, courthouse bums, pimps, loafers and thieves numbering about 4000.

The theory was that Torrio had had Colosimo taken care of to get more money for himself by taking control of the rackets. The police believed that Torrio had imported Frankie Uale, the New York head of the *Unione Siciliana*, to commit the murder. Then Torrio told Colosimo that two truckloads of liquor would soon arrive at Colosimo's restaurant. Big Jim went there to receive the shipment and received a fusillade of bullets – of course, from the usual unknown assailant.

Right: Chicago Federal Agents survey distilling equipment and whiskey that they have just confiscated.

Opposite left: Agents dumping whiskey after a raid.

Opposite right: A 1930 photograph of a speakeasy at 2837 South Michigan Avenue.

Below: Chief Deputy United States Marshal Sam Howard (left) directs the burning of more than 1000 beer and wine kegs at the municipal dump at 34th Street and Kedzie Avenue – 21 November 1924.

The previous year Torrio had become vexed because Colosimo had seemed to be tiring of the business, so he had sent to his Alma Mater, the Five Points Gang in New York, for a chief of staff. He ended up with a bullet-headed 23-year-old Neapolitan roughneck named Al Capone. Capone (also known as Al Brown) was in trouble with the law in New York and was glad to go to Chicago as a bodyguard and chauffeur for Torrio. Capone got a salary and half the profits of the bootleg trade.

By that time Torrio had had an idea. He had discovered that there was big money in the illegal liquor business, and he wanted to control the dispensation of booze to the whole city of Chicago. Of course, he had competition, but if he had a small army of men, handy with fists and guns, he could pull it off by intimidating rival bootleggers and

Opposite top: A 1931 Chicago rogue's gallery print of Al Capone.

Left: In order to hide her two tins of liquor, this woman wore a floppy overcoat.

Opposite bottom: Another woman had a similar idea – hide the whiskey in floppy boots.

Below: Johnny Torrio, the king of crime on the South Side of Chicago during the 1920s.

using persuasion on the proprietors of speakeasies, joints that were sometimes referred to as 'Blind Pigs.' Capone set himself up in Torrio's gambling place, The Four Deuces, and had cards printed up that read: Alphonse Capone/Second Hand Furniture Dealer/2220 South Wabash Avenue.

In 1923 Chicago elected an honest mayor to replace Bill Thompson – Judge William E Dever – who closed so many speakeasies that Torrio moved his operations to suburban Cicero. In 1924 Capone used his goons so adroitly that only candidates who favored a wide-open Cicero were elected to office. Soon Cicero, a town of only 50,000 inhabitants, had more than 150 speakeasies.

The Chicago gangs often argued over territorial rights, especially the Torrio mob and Dion O'Banion's North Side organization. In 1924 Torrio was caught by the police while he was directing the loading of his liquor trucks. O'Banion was also arrested, but Torrio later learned that it was O'Banion who had tipped off the raiders. Torrio had given O'Banion a part of the Cicero beer business to keep down the violence, but then O'Banion complained that Torrio's friends, the Genna Brothers, had made incursions into the North Side. Torrio didn't do anything about the situation, and that was why O'Banion had told the police about Torrio's ownership of a brewery, which resulted in Torrio's arrest. It netted him a $5000 fine and a nine-months' jail sentence.

Below: Rocco Fanelli, one of Al Capone's bodyguards, was jailed as a suspect in the St Valentine's Day Massacre. Fanelli did not wait to be captured but tried to turn himself in. He walked into police headquarters but was told to come back later, which he did.

Dion O'Banion, a former choir boy, ran the North Side, and referred to Torrio and Capone as 'Guinea bastards,' spitting whenever anyone mentioned their names. O'Banion was probably the most picturesque of the Chicago gang leaders, and he was the last important Irish-American criminal in Chicago history. It was alleged that he had killed 25 men. He also controlled the votes of the 42nd and 43rd Wards at election time – usually delivering them for the Democrats, but in 1924 to the Republicans to help ensure Bill Thompson's re-election.

O'Banion, a complex character, was a gangster by night and a florist by day – a connoisseur of orchids and murder. On 10 November 1924, O'Banion was busy in his flower shop opposite Holy Name Cathedral, working on a giant floral bleeding heart for the funeral of Mike Merola, a lieutenant of Torrio's who had died of natural causes (a rare thing at the time).

Three men got out of a car in front of his shop and came through the door. O'Banion, thinking that they were Torrio's henchmen, Albert Anselmi, John Scalisi and Mike Genna, come to pick up the bleeding heart (which had been ordered by Capone), walked through the door to meet them. The middle man of the three shook hands with O'Banion – and held on while six bullets were fired into O'Banion's body. Talk about the kiss of Judas. The three men climbed into the sedan and left the scene. They were never arrested.

O'Banion had an expensive gangster-style funeral – a $10,000 casket, 26 open automobiles filled with flowers, including one basket which bore the touching inscription 'From Al.' Forty thousand people had viewed the body (O'Banion's buttonhole carnation was replaced every hour). Ten thousand people were in the funeral procession and

Above: Cook County Sheriff Peter M Hoffman (left) and an assistant, LeRoy Davidson, in the County Building vault where they secretly stockpiled confiscated liquor. Even while Hoffman was serving 30 days in the Wheaton jail, Davidson, the chief of the highway police, went on collecting the booze.

when they arrived at the gravesite, they were met by 10,000 other mourners.

Hymie Weiss inherited O'Banion's operations. Accompanied by two of his mobsters, Bugs Moran and Schemer Drucci, on 12 January 1925, he fired on Capone's car at the intersection of State and 55th Streets. But Capone was not in the car, and only the driver was wounded. Twelve days later, two North Side gangsters put five bullets in Torrio's body, but he recovered to serve his nine months in jail.

The Weiss mob was sure that O'Banion had been killed by some of the six Genna Brothers from the West Side, on orders from Torrio and Capone. O'Banion had also been feuding with the Gennas. Suddenly Gennas started dropping like flies – dying of what, for them, were natural causes. Angelo was killed in May 1925, Anthony in June and Michael in July. The remaining three, Sam, Jim and Pete, escaped to Sicily.

When Johnny Torrio was released from jail, he felt that he had had enough. He retired and went back to Italy, probably taking some $30,000,000 with him. This left the 26-year-old Capone as top man.

He inherited a chain of roadhouses where prostitutes were available and beer and whiskey were sold 24 hours a day. The payroll for his personal staff came to $1,600,000 per year, plus a huge sum to pay off politicians and policemen. He also paid an illegal brewery $1,000,000 per month for its product. Federal investigators estimated that his enterprises had a gross income of $70,000,000 per year. He rode around in a chauffeur-driven car that weighed seven tons. It was bullet-proof and had combination locks on the doors. He was able to rationalize his actions by saying, 'I make my money by supplying a public demand. If I break the law, my customers, who number hundreds of the best people in Chicago, are as guilty as I am. The only difference between us is that I sell and they buy.'

By the use of bribery and violence, Capone was able to move into Chicago Heights, Blue Island, Blue Oaks, Stickney, Forest View and other Cook County towns south and southwest of Chicago, changing them, as one minister said, 'from peaceful suburbs into brothel-ridden Babylons.' Meantime, he had Cicero all to himself.

Originally, a West Side gangster named Klondike O'Donnell was the supplier of beer

Above: Terry Duggan's Brewery at 12th Street and Oakley Avenue was running full blast even in 1930.

Opposite top: The Angelo Genna funeral was a splendid affair.

and liquor for Cicero. He worked with his brother Myles and two politicians, Eddie Vogel and Eddie Tancl. When Capone's takeover was accomplished, the O'Donnells accepted positions in the Capone mob, but Tancl did not, so Myles picked a fight with him and shot him dead.

Capone was acquiring a sort of finesse in the management of politicians. In 1925 he had control of Cicero and had put his own mayor in office. He had his own agents in the gambling houses and the 161 bars, and a lavish headquarters in the Hawthorn Hotel on 22nd Street. The headquarters had steel-shuttered windows and electrically operated doors. There were 700 men in Capone's army, many of them experts with the sawed-off shotgun and the Thompson submachine gun.

Capone really ran the town. Once he publicly upbraided the mayor of Cicero, Joseph Z Klenka, threw him down the City Hall steps and kicked him when he tried to get up from the sidewalk. He broke up meetings of the Town Council and silenced critics and newspaper editors with his blackjack.

In 1926 Assistant State's Attorney William H McSwiggin was found murdered on a Cicero street. He had been the enemy of the South Side O'Donnells – no relation to Klondike and Myles – four brothers who were rivals of Capone. There were those who thought that Capone had arranged the murder to make it look as though the O'Donnells had done it. At any rate, he drove them out of business and took over the whole South Side himself.

Then began years of wild and senseless gang warfare. Often the victim would be 'taken for a ride.' The technique was to lure the victim into a car, shoot him at leisure, drive to a distant part of the city and dump his body. Or a room or an apartment could be rented – one overlooking the victim's front door. When he came out of his dwelling he could be sprayed with machine-gun bullets. Another technique was to steal a car and man it with hoods armed with shotguns and submachine guns, draw up beside the rival's car, force him to the curb, open fire, get lost in the traffic and abandon the stolen car.

On 20 September 1926, Hymie Weiss staged an incident in broad daylight. While the streets of Cicero were alive with heavy traffic, the North Siders drove eight touring cars past Capone's headquarters – spitting machine-gun fire from each car. Capone flung himself flat on the floor of the Hawthorn Hotel restaurant and lived to tell the tale. But at least the Weiss gangsters were gentlemen. The first car's executioners shot blank cartridges to disperse the innocent bystanders.

A few weeks later Weiss was gunned down near Holy Name Cathedral. He was succeeded by Drucci, who was soon killed in a

Opposite bottom: The funeral services for William McSwiggin were held at St Thomas Aquinas Roman Catholic Church at 5112 Washington Boulevard, on the corner of Lexington Avenue.

Right: Frank Lake (left) and Terrance Druggan, two prominent beer runners, who were able to get out of Cook County jail almost whenever they pleased. The permissiveness of the jailers led to a federal investigation.

gunfight with the police. Then Bugs Moran took over the North Side. And Bugs was having trouble with the Capone mob.

Not until St Valentine's Day of 1929 did the gang war reach its climax. At 10:30 AM on 14 February, seven men were sitting in a garage of the S M C Cartage Company at 2122 North Clark Street, waiting for a load of hijacked liquor. Six of them were members of Bugs Moran's mob and the other was an innocent bystander. Three men dressed as police officers got out of a Cadillac touring car, followed by two others in civilian dress. The three 'policemen' came into the garage, disarmed the six gangsters, who thought that they were really law officers, and told the seven men to stand in a row facing the wall. The mobsters were used to police raids, and they knew that they would get off easily enough. But then the two civilians came in and machine-gunned them down – all seven of them. The fake policemen pretended to arrest the two civilians, marched them to the car and drove off. True to the gangster's code, however, when asked who shot him, the

162

MENS CELLROOM

Right: On 22 November 1927 the Chicago police raided a room in the Atlantic Hotel in the Loop and found some gangsters who had been imported from New York, St Louis and San Francisco to serve in the gang wars that year. Also found were machine guns trained on a cigar store across the street, which was frequented by Al Capone and Antonio Lombardo, leader of the Unione Siciliana. Rounded up were, left to right: Michael Bizarro, Joseph Aiello (leader of an anti-Capone gang), Joseph Rubinello, Jack Monzello and Joseph Russio.

Opposite top: Chicago even had a sacramental wine racket, which poured 3 million gallons of champagne, port, sherry and muscatel into bootleg channels in three years, earning the racketeers more than $15 million, while lining the pockets of members of the Prohibition Board with another $1 million. Left to right: Patrick Roche, a federal special intelligence agent, who discovered the racket, and Edward Peifer and Lee Klein, assistant US district attorneys.

Below: In 1929 the Chicago police were phasing out their motorcycles and replacing them with Ford squad cars.

dying Frank Gusenberg said, 'Nobody shot me,' Moran said, 'Only Capone kills like that.'

Three of the killers were alleged to be John Scalisi, Joseph Guinta and Albert Anselmi, who were found dead in Douglas Park three months later. There were two theories about this triple murder, but there was no question that Capone had had second thoughts about the St Valentine's Day Massacre. One theory was that Capone had ratted on the three to Bugs Moran, who sought them out and had them killed. The other theory was that the three had been invited to a Capone banquet, after which he knocked in their heads with a baseball bat. The bodies had been riddled with bullets as well as being thoroughly smashed to pulp.

In the 1920s there were over 500 gang murders in all, and few of the murderers were apprehended. The reasons were that the killings were carefully planned, bribe money changed hands, witnesses were intimidated and no gangster would testify against another.

Toward the end of the decade, Capone was making a lot of money. He controlled revenues from alcohol of $60 million; most of it came from beer. He controlled the sale of liquor to 10,000 speakeasies, and he also controlled the sources of supply as far away as Canada and the Florida Coast. He was making $25 million per year from gambling establishments and dog tracks. Vice, dance halls, roadhouses and resorts returned another $10 million. Federal agents estimated his personal fortune at around $20 million.

Capone lived high and was well protected. When he was on the streets, he was always preceded by another car and followed by yet another containing his armed henchmen. When he went to the theater, he went with a bodyguard of 18 goons. And he was barely 30 years old.

An observer of the scene at the time said:

Chicago seemed to be filled with gangsters –

gangsters slaughtering one another, two hundred and fifteen in four years; gangsters being killed by the police, one hundred and sixty in the same length of time; gangsters shooting up saloons for amusement; gangsters throwing bombs called 'pineapples'; gangsters improving their marks manship on machine-gun ranges in sparsely settled neighborhoods; gangsters speeding in big auto-mobiles, ignoring traffic laws; gangsters strutting in the Loop, holstered pistols scarcely concealed; gangsters giving orders to the police, to judges, to prosecutors, all sworn to uphold the law; gangsters calling on their friends and protectors at City Hall and the County Courthouse; gangsters dining in expensive restaurants and cafés; tuxe-doed gangsters at the opera and the theater, their mink-coated, Paris-gowned wives or sweethearts on their arms; gangsters entertaining politicians and city officials at 'Belshazzar feasts,' some of which cost twenty-five thousand dollars; gang-sters giving parties at which the guests playfully doused each other with champagne at twenty dollars a bottle, popping a thousand corks in a single evening; and all with huge bankrolls – a gangster with less than five thousand dollars in his pocket was a rarity.

It wasn't only Prohibition, or rather the public's refusal to abide by it, that was to blame. Blame the automobile that made escape easy. Blame the adaptation to peace-time use of weapons. Blame the importation

of Mafia killers. Blame the sheer size of Chicago, where, as in any other huge city, people don't get excited about things that do not directly affect them. Blame the apathy (everywhere) of the times.

Capone now seemed to have everthing under control. Where else was there to turn in Chicago to make more money? The protec-tion racket: a scheme for collecting cash from businessmen to 'protect' them from damage.

Below: The merchants on Maxwell Street in Chicago's Jewish ghetto complained bitterly that they were having to pay too much to the mobs in the protection racket.

And who would provide the damage? The mob, of course. The victim soon learned that if he did not pay off, his shop would be bombed or he would be shot. Even the most respectable shop owners would think 'I can't change suppliers or I will have both my legs broken.' There was no recourse, since the authorities were fixed, or at least frightened.

One of the biggest rackets in Chicago was the cleaners and dyers' racket; it controlled the proprietors so completely that it could raise the price of having a suit cleaned from $1.25 to $1.75 overnight. One of the more clever ways of intimidation was to have explosive chemicals sewed to the seams of trousers sent to be cleaned.

There was also the garage racket, thought up by David Albin, aka 'Cockeye Mulligan.' A garage owner had to join the 'Mid-West Garage Association' or his garage would be bombed, his mechanics would be beaten up, or cars in the garage would be destroyed.

There was the window-washing racket, too. Every time a man wanted to open a window-washing company, he had to pay off the hoods.

In 1929 there were, according to the State's

Then the unpleasant word got around. Everyone knew that Capone liked his name in the paper and that reporters needed information – especially police reporters. And everyone knew that Lingle was the police reporter closest to Capone. But Lingle did live rather high for a man who was making a paltry $65 per week at the paper.

The *Tribune* learned that Lingle had a suite, at the Morrison Hotel, a house on the West

Above: A 1933 photograph of 'Machine Gun' Jack McGurn.

Opposite top: This soup kitchen at 935 South State Street was maintained by Al Capone himself.

Opposite bottom: The new Illinois Central tunnel at Van Buren and Michigan in 1925. It was near here that Alfred 'Jake' Lingle was gunned down.

Far right: Joseph Aiello.

Attorney's Office, 91 rackets in Chicago. Seventy-five of them were in active operation, and it was costing the citizens about $136,000,000 per year.

The favorite weapon of the racketeer was the bomb. A bomber doing a routine job with a black-powder bomb would charge $100. A risky job with a dynamite bomb would cost $1000. From 11 October 1927 to 15 January 1928, 157 bombs were set or exploded in Chicago, and none of the bombers was arrested. By the end of the 1920s, businessmen were turning to Al Capone for protection from the protection rackets.

Chicago was stunned by another murder in 1930. Alfred 'Jake' Lingle was a *Chicago Tribune* police reporter, a man-about-town and an authority on gangsters. On 9 July Lingle left his desk at the Criminal Courts Building on Randolph Street about 1:00 PM and made for the race track. He was gunned down in the underground approach to the Illinois Central Suburban Station near the Chicago Public Library.

It was first thought that Lingle had been killed because of his newspaper connections, and the *Tribune* offered a $25,000 reward.

Right: All Chicago went on a party when Prohibition was repealed.

Below: Empty shelves in this liquor store marked the first legal sales of spirits after Prohibition ended.

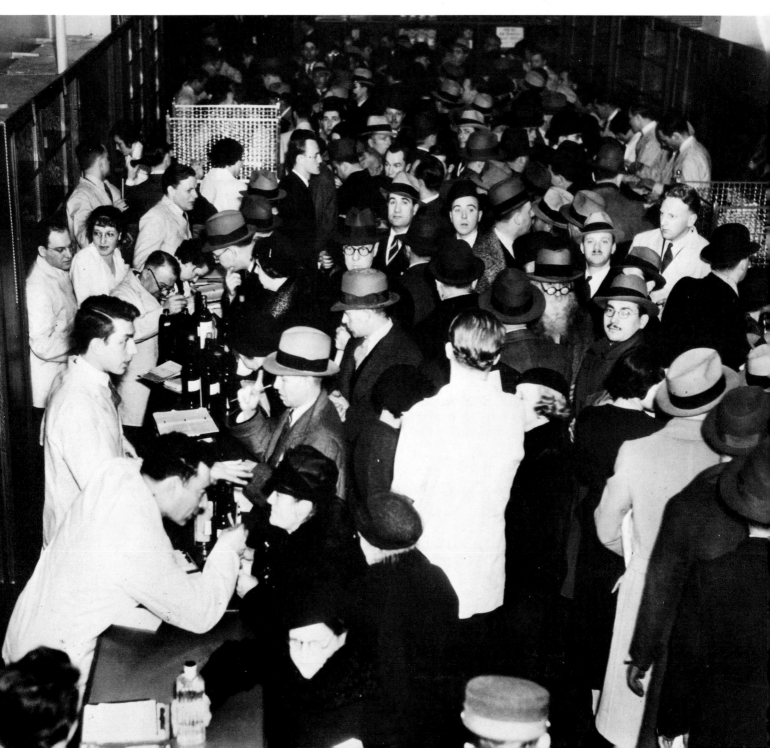

Left: A truck leaving the *Chicago Daily Times* office during that paper's campaign against Al Capone.

Side and a summer home in Wisconsin. He wore tailor-made suits and English shoes. He bet big money at the race tracks day after day. He had an active account of $100,000 average at his stockbroker's. He had bank accounts in the thousands. He obviously knew how to make a dollar go a long way.

Suddenly Lingle ceased to be a martyr. He had been called 'the unofficial police chief of Chicago.' And now it was said that among his friends, in addition to Capone, 'he counted Police Commissioner William F Russell and enough minor police officials, judges and politicians to fill a garbage scow.'

It turned out that Lingle was setting the price of beer in Chicago; he controlled the graft from dog racing and took a hand in the closing and later reopening of gambling houses. Lingle's high police contacts resigned from the force.

A St Louis hoodlum named Leo Brothers was convicted of the one-shot-to-the-brain killing and was given a 14-year sentence, getting off for good behavior after 10 years. There are those who thought that Jack Zuta of the Bugs Moran gang had arranged the murder, but Zuta died by gunfire on 1 August 1930 at a roadhouse in the Wisconsin woods. Records indicate that Moran had lost money in the closing of a Sheridan Road gambling house, blaming Lingle for the trouble. Perhaps he had also had Zuta killed to keep him quiet.

Capone vowed revenge for the killing of Lingle, but never did anything about it. He had other things to worry about. For example, on 26 August 1930 he was playing golf with City Sealer Dan Serritella and a nearby truck backfired. Scarface thought it was gunfire and jumped into a sand trap while his bodyguards, 'Greasy Thumb' Guzik and Hymie Levine, pulled their weapons from their golf bags. The incident made the front page of the *Chicago Daily News*. Obviously, Capone was worried. And the heat was coming from both sides – the underworld and the police.

John Stege, an honest police captain who had often been transferred to inconvenient posts because of his relentless pressure on Capone, was brought back to the Central Office and immediately put a constant surveillance on the mobster. Meanwhile, the Treasury Department was building a federal tax-evasion case against him. Capone was indicted in the early autumn of 1931, convicted and sentenced to eight years in a federal penitentiary. He left Alcatraz a broken man and died of a venereal disease in Florida at his secluded estate.

After the repeal of Prohibition in 1933, Chicago hotels began blossoming with cocktail lounges, taprooms and bars. They boasted chromium fittings, large mirrors, bright-colored furniture, venetian blinds and bartenders who came over from the speakeasies.

Below: The instruments found in the home of James J Probasco at 2509 North Crawford Avenue were said to be the ones used to create a new face for bank robber John Dillinger. While he was being questioned in the offices of government agents, Probasco leaped out of a 19th floor window and plunged to his death.

These bartenders brought back the Bronx and Jack Rose cocktails to go with the martinis and manhattans. Night clubs and supper clubs opened. Liquor stores proliferated. Private clubs and fraternal lodges noticed a falling off of membership, attributable to the increased coeducational social patterns to be found in legal drinking places.

Some bootleggers became legitimate, and some of them went into the rackets. Some became unemployed and some went on bootlegging. The Federal Government had put such high taxes on liquor that bootlegging still could be profitable, and illegal booze sales did not start to decline until 1938. Some estimates indicated that in 1934 and 1935, 60 percent of the liquor consumed in the United States was illegal.

The Depression had also spawned the bank

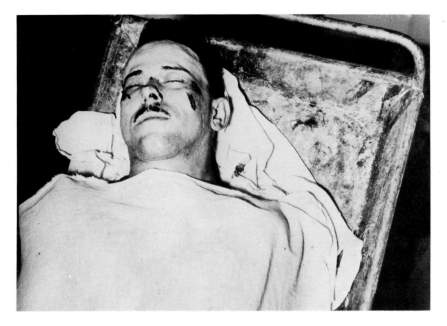

Above: The corpse of John Dillinger.

Opposite top: The living room in the apartment of Anna Sage (The Lady in Red) on North Halsted Street, where Dillinger spent a good many leisure hours.

Opposite: The usual swarm of curious spectators surrounds John Dillinger's hearse as it leaves the mortuary at 4506 Sheridan Road with the body of the slain desperado.

Far right: Mrs Anna Sage.

robber. John Dillinger was a bank robber and hold-up man who had a talent for shooting his way out of difficulty. This man from Indiana had bungled one hold-up and, while in prison, formed a gang of fellow convicts. He broke out of the Crown Point jail in Lake County, Indiana, by using a wooden gun and some non-wooden money. And he continued to rob banks.

Many viewed Dillinger as a hero – he was robbing the banks that had robbed the common man after the Crash in 1929. State and local police could do little to stop him, and J Edgar Hoover, the head of the Federal Bureau of Investigation of the Department of Justice, saw his chance. Of course, Dillinger had but one federal offense against him – the interstate transportation of a stolen car – but that made no difference. Now that Capone was in jail, Hoover made Dillinger Public Enemy Number One. G-Men went on the job of trying to take him. They tried to take him in St Paul, Minnesota, and at a resort named Little Bohemia, in northern Wisconsin near Mercer, but he escaped by shooting his way out.

On the evening of 22 July 1934, a group of agents from the Department of Justice, led by G-Man Melvin Purvis, met in Chicago. Armed with pistols, they gathered around the Biograph movie house on Lincoln Avenue, near the intersection of Lincoln and Fullerton Avenues and Halsted Street. The movie playing that night was *Manhattan Melodrama*, starring Clark Gable, William Powell, Myrna Loy and Mickey Rooney. Ironically, it was the story of two boyhood pals who grow up together in the slums. One of them becomes a district attorney and the other becomes a criminal.

Purvis parked his car near the door of the theater and looked at the faces of the men and women who entered. Finally he recognized the man he wanted, although this man had dyed his hair, had had his face lifted, had grown a moustache and was wearing gold-rimmed glasses. The clue was that Dillinger was accompanied by a traitor called 'The Lady in Red.' Her name was Anna Sage, and she was no lady and didn't wear red, but she had promised to finger Dillinger for the FBI to avoid deportation. (She was eventually deported anyway.)

Purvis and his men waited for two hours until the first show was over and the man reappeared. The G-Man signaled to his aids by putting his arm out of the car window, lowering his hand and closing it into a fist. The men closed in on the criminal, and when he drew an automatic, they shot him down. John Dillinger, Public Enemy Number One, was dead.

Some of the more bloodthirsty people in the neighborhood, when they found out who had been killed, ran to the spot and mopped up spilled blood with their handkerchiefs. They gouged some of the wayward bullets from the wooden telephone pole near the theater. Later, when Dillinger was buried, others went to the cemetery and took chips from his tombstone. This tombstone can be seen today in the Dillinger Museum in Nashville, Indiana – his home town.

SPORTS AND GAMES

Chicago had always been sports-mad, and the Glamour Years were no exception. People on the North Side were Cub fans. People on the South Side were White Sox fans. People on the West Side had their choice. The baseball teams were the most important thing in the world.

Then came professional football. The Bears played in the Cubs' Wrigley Field and the Cardinals played in the Sox' Comiskey Park. And even in the days when no Chicago native had ever tried that strange sport from north of the border, the Black Hawks were selling out their hockey games.

One of the most exciting boxing matches of all time was held in Chicago – the second Dempsey-Tunney fight in 1927. It took place in Chicago's International Amphitheater at the Union Stock Yards, an arena so big that it was estimated that two-thirds of the people in the outermost seats didn't know who had won when the fight was over. It was claimed that more than 40,000,000 people heard it on the radio. This was the celebrated long-count fight. During the seventh round, Gene Tunney was knocked down and the referee delayed beginning the count until Jack Dempsey got a neutral corner, giving Tunney 13 seconds to recover. Tunney then climbed off the canvas and won the fight. Reports say that five people in the United States dropped dead of heart failure at their radios.

Tennis and golf were beginning to catch on in Chicago in the early 1920s, but the big rage began in 1930 - miniature golf. Thousands of people were parking their cars by half-acre courses and earnestly knocking golf balls along the cottonseed fairways, through little mouse holes in wooden barricades, over little bridges and through drainpipes, while the proprietors listened happily to the tinkle of the cash register. It was said that some of the courses reported profits of 300 percent a month.

In 1931 and 1932, factories often went to the five-day week to spread the work around. It was the same in offices. The result was new leisure. Another result was the softball craze that developed. And with extra time at their disposal, people could also watch some professional sports.

One of the first ballplayers to return to the Cubs after World War I was the phenomenal pitcher Grover Cleveland Alexander. But he was not the man that he had been. Under the constant shelling of trench warfare, Alexander had lost his hearing in one ear and developed epilepsy. Like many players of the era, he was a heavy drinker, but after the war his drinking increased to epic proportions, largely, it is now supposed, as a mask for his problems.

At the time, alcoholism was more socially acceptable than epilepsy, and it seems that much of the erratic behavior attributed to Alexander's drinking was actually caused by his illness.

Alexander was never to return to the heights of his previous achievement, but it is a tribute to his extraordinary natural ability that he remained an effective pitcher after the war, and three times won at least 21 games in the hit-happy 1920s. He was traded to the St Louis Cardinals in 1926.

Under the stewardship of former minor-league infielder Joe McCarthy, the Cubs beat out the second-place Pittsburgh Pirates by 10-½ games in 1929, the first of nine pennants for McCarthy and the first flag since 1918 for the Chicago Cubs. As more and more life was pumped into the ball, batting averages continued to swell and balls continued to fly out of the ball parks. The Cubs' winning outfield of Kiki Cuyler, Hack Wilson and Riggs Stephenson batted .360, .345 and .362, respectively.

Rogers Hornsby, 'the Rajah,' now on second base for the Cubs, traded the previous November by the St Louis Cardinals, hit 40 homers, drove in 149 runs and racked up a .380 average, for which he received his second Most Valuable Player Award. Not bad for an outlay of five players and $200,000 in cash.

In 1930 six clubs, because of the ever-pumped-up ball, posted team batting averages of over .300 – the Chicago Cubs, the New York Giants, the Philadelphia Phillies, the St Louis Cardinals, the Brooklyn Dodgers and the Pittsburgh Pirates. That was

Previous pages: The 1919 Chicago White Sox, winners of the American League pennant and owners of the dismal nickname of the Black Sox.

Below: Gene Tunney on the deck, taking his long count, in the championship fight in Chicago in 1927.

six teams out of the eight that were in the National League. Leading the pack in individual hitting was Chicago's stubby, hard-drinking outfielder Louis 'Hack' Wilson, with 190 runs batted in – a major league record that may never be broken – and 56 home runs – a National League record that still stands.

In 1931, despite Wilson's unremarkable 13 home runs and 129 fewer RBIs than his record of the previous year, the Cubs led the league with a team average of .289. That was good enough, since, over the winter, the team owners had squeezed some of the juice out of the lively ball.

In 1932 Rogers Hornsby was the manager of the Cubs: he was fired with the team in first place on 2 August, after a series of vitriolic policy disputes with Cub President William Veeck Sr. Charlie Grimm, who was later to be known as the best banjo player in the National League, replaced him, and the Cubs went on to take the pennant, beating out Pittsburgh by four games. The team demonstrated its opinion of Hornsby by not voting him a share in the World Series money.

Above: The running of the American Derby at Washington Park, 1935.

Left: The immortal Gallant Fox, with the equally immortal Earl Sande up – Washington Park, 1930.

174

The Giants and the Cardinals ran a close pennant race in 1935, the Giants leading most of the way. But the Cubs sneaked up on them, taking the lead and winning the pennant with a historic winning streak – they won their last 21 games of the season. Chicago pitchers Bill Lee and Lon Warneke were both 20-game winners, and second baseman Billy Herman hit .341. The great Casey Stengel contributed

Below: William 'Billy' Herman, the great Cub infielder of the 1930s.

an anecdote to the baseball archives after his Dodgers, in a display of exquisite bumbling, ended a four-game winning streak by dropping a double header to the Cubs. As the Brooklyn manager climbed into a Chicago barber chair, he announced, 'A shave, please, but don't cut my throat. I may want to do it myself later.'

A classic pennant race drama that ended in a famous home run took place in late September of 1938, when the Cubs met the Pirates in Wrigley Field for a three-game series to settle the championship. The Pirates enjoyed a one-and-a-half-game lead before leaving for Chicago, but in the opening game the sore-armed Dizzy Dean beat them 2-1. The next day's game was still tied in the bottom of the ninth inning. With darkness gathering, it seemed likely that the game would be called a tie and replayed as a part of a double header the next day. With two out, the Cubs' catcher, Gabby Hartnett, who had also been the manager since July, came to bat. After two strikes in the fading light, he connected on a fast ball thrown by Mace Brown, and hit his immortal 'homer in the gloamin', winning the game. Now half a game up, the Cubs trounced the dispirited Pirates the next day 10-1, to win the pennant as they had in 1929, 1932 and 1935, on a weird three-year schedule. But again they failed to win the World Series, as had happened since 1929. The Yankees devoured them, winning four straight.

Even if the Cubs couldn't win a World Series, things were worse on the South Side.

The year 1919 stands out in baseball history, but not for good reasons. It was the year of the White Sox Scandal, or, rather, the Black Sox Scandal. White Sox owner Charles Comiskey's team had a reputation for being outstanding – when they wanted to be. The problem was gambling, and after winning the pennant they threw the 1919 World Series to the Cincinnati Reds. Thus came the title of 'Black Sox.'

Eight players were involved in the scandal: outfielder 'Shoeless Joe' Jackson, third baseman George 'Buck' Weaver, first baseman Arnold 'Chick' Gandil, shortstop Charles 'Swede' Risberg, pitchers Eddie Cicotte and Claude 'Lefty' Williams, center fielder Oscar 'Happy' Felsch and utility infielder Fred McMullin. Sox star Eddie Collins was one of those who remained untainted.

The Sox had reportedly been split into cliques for some time, the split being along the lines of who was crooked and who was straight. Weaver, it was held by some, was guilty only by association, having sat in on the negotiations for the fix although he decided not to participate in it.

The ringleaders were Cicotte, Gandil and Williams, who approached the gamblers (including the notorious Arnold Rothstein) in New York in midseason to set the stakes. The players were promised $100,000, most of

which they were never to see. It must have seemed like a lot of money in those days, when a player was doing well if he earned $6000. Comiskey contributed to the trouble in the sense that he was notoriously tight, paying the lowest salaries in either major league.

Betting odds before the Series began went from 3-1 in favor of the White Sox to 8-5 in favor of Cincinnati, a sure clue to the shenanigans going on. The pre-established high sign was for the White Sox pitcher to hit the first batter in the first game. Eddie Cicotte performed on cue, and Cincinnati won the game, 9-1.

Claude Williams walked the three batters in a single inning in the second game, an unheard-of feat for him, and the Reds won again, this time 4-2. When Comiskey got wind of what was going on, he passed the word on to John Heydler, the president of the National League, who informed Ban Johnson, president of the American League. Johnson, who by now had fallen out with Comiskey in a personal feud, dismissed it as 'the yelp of a beaten cur.'

The Sox won the third game 3-0, possibly because the gamblers were reneging on their promise to pay the ballplayers $10,000 of the $100,000 total after each game. Two errors by Cicotte gave the Reds a 2-0 win in the fourth game, and they won again, 5-0, in the fifth. The Series had been temporarily lengthened

Opposite right: Charlie Grimm of the Cubs and Mickey Cochrane of the Tigers – rival managers in the World Series.

Below left: Joe McCarthy, who managed the Cubs and built a small dynasty.

Below: 'Shoeless Joe' Jackson and 'Happy' Felsch of the White Sox.

Left: The lawyers who defended Charles Comiskey when he was sued by 'Shoeless Joe' Jackson for a mere $18,500 after the Black Sox scandal.

Right: The great Eddie Collins of the Chicago White Sox.

to a best of nine that year, so the Reds needed one more win to take the Series.

Cicotte talked manager Kid Gleason into letting him pitch again, and the Sox won 4-1. Then Claude Williams lost to the Reds and the series was over. It had broken all records in receipts and attendance, and the Reds were the first team in baseball history to earn more than $5000 apiece in World Series money. Nothing was said publicly about the fix until the following September, but rumors flew fast and furious. Boxer Abe Attell confessed to being involved in the deal and named the eight players. The *Chicago Tribune* called for a grand jury investigation. When confronted by Gleason and Comiskey, Cicotte broke down. He, Jackson and Williams gave the details of how the games were rigged to a grand jury, and Comiskey suspended all eight. As 'Shoeless Joe' Jackson was leaving the courthouse after the grand jury hearing, a small boy supposedly came up to him with tears in his eyes, and, as the legend goes, said, 'Say it ain't so, Joe.'

Criminal indictments followed, but by then the players' written confessions had disappeared, and they were all acquitted. According to the letter of the law, they could have been reinstated.

But the brand-new Commissioner of Baseball, Judge Kennesaw Mountain Landis (named for a battle of the Civil War) took quick and decisive action. 'Regardless of the verdict of juries, no player that throws a game, no player that entertains proposals or promises to throw a game, no player that sits in conference with a bunch of crooks and gamblers where the ways and means of

Above: Judge Kennesaw Mountain Landis, the first Commissioner of Baseball, who saved the game after the scandal.

Opposite bottom: Charles 'The Old Roman' Comiskey, the owner of the White Sox and the man for whom Comiskey Park is named.

throwing games are discussed, and does not promptly tell his club about it, will ever play professional baseball.'

The Black Sox Scandal seriously undermined the confidence of many in the game that had become the national pastime, but Landis's firm handling of the scandal helped mitigate the disgrace. Some felt that some of the players deserved a pardon. Buck Weaver, for example, never shared in the ill-gained profits, and played .324 ball in the Series. Ten thousand fans signed a petition calling for his reinstatement, but Judge Landis sternly turned a cold shoulder.

'Shoeless Joe' Jackson got no fix money either, and averaged .375 for the Series, the best in either league, but he was never allowed back into baseball. In fact, when word got back to Judge Landis that Jackson had been hired to coach a Class-D minor league team, Landis ordered him fired. It took the legendary Babe Ruth to wipe the slate clean in the Roaring Twenties and make the crowds forget about the dirty deeds their heroes in Chicago had done, and the Sox were not to win another pennant until 1959, when they lost the Series 4-2 to the Los Angeles Dodgers.

Chicago was also responsible for another baseball institution – The All-Star Game. Sports editor Arch Ward of the *Chicago Tribune* thought up the idea as a way of publicising the city during its first World's Fair year of 1933. The American League beat the National League team 4-2, and the tradition remains.

World War I must be given some credit for the formation of modern professional foot-

Above: 'Red' Grange of the Chicago Bears runs the ball against the New York Giants.

Below: The 1933 National League All-Star Team, whose All-Star Game that year was the first ever. Dreamed up by Arch Ward, the sports editor of the *Chicago Tribune*, it was played at Comiskey Park.

ball, for it was at the Rose Bowl Game of 1918 that a team representing the Great Lakes Naval Training Station (just up the road from Chicago) trounced the Mare Island Marines squad. On the Great Lakes team were some of the men who were to shape major league football. George Halas, fresh from the University of Illinois, played end. Jim Conselman, John 'Paddy' Driscoll and Harold Erickson were in the backfield. Hugh Blacklock, Jerry Jones and Emmett Keefe were also on the team.

The National Football League was conceived in July 1919 in Canton, Ohio. Five teams signed up that day and all of them remained in the league, at least until 1925. The meeting was held in Ralph Hays's auto agency, and the league looked like this: the Akron Pros (owned by Frank Neid); the Canton, Ohio, Bulldogs (Ralph Hays); the Columbus, Ohio, Panhandles (Joe Carr); the Dayton, Ohio, Triangles (Carl Storck); the Rochester, New York, Jeffersons (Leo Lyons). They decided to call themselves the American Professional Football Association, and the franchise fee was $25.

Several teams were added for the 1919 season – the Cleveland Indians, the Detroit Heralds, the Hammond (Indiana) Pros, the Massilon (Ohio) Tigers, the Rock Island (Illinois) Independents, the Toledo Maroons and a team from Wheeling, West Virginia. In 1920 the league was joined (at a $100 price this time) by the Decatur (Illinois) Staleys, who were named for the Staley Starch Company of owner A E Staley; the Racine (Wisconsin) Cardinals; the Buffalo (New York) All Americans; the Chicago Tigers and the Cleveland Panthers.

In 1921 the Staleys and the Cardinals had moved to Chicago and George Halas, who

Above: 'The Galloping Ghost,' 'Red' Grange, runs for a long gain as a Chicago Bear.

now owned the Staleys, won his first league championship, beating the Green Bay Packers (playing under the banner of the Acme Packing Company) by a score of 20-0.

The League changed its name to the National Football League in 1922 and the Staleys became the Chicago Bears and came in second to the Canton Bulldogs. On the Bears' team was Halas's old teammate, Hugh Black-lock, playing tackle. The Chicago Cardinals finished just behind the Bears in third place in an 18-team league. They were coached by 'Paddy' Driscoll.

The Bears were second again in 1923 in a 20-team league, and the Cardinals finished sixth. In 1924 the Bears were second again and the Cards were ninth.

The turning point for the whole league occurred in 1925 when Halas signed Harold 'Red' Grange, who was the most outstanding college football player in the country when he played for the University of Illinois. He start-ed for the Bears on 26 November, after his college season was over, and collected $12,000. But he was worth it. Grange pulled in 36,000 fans in his first game in Wrigley Field, when the Bears played the Cardinals. The next week, he drew 28,000 fans for a game against the Columbus Tigers. Even so, the Cardinals won the title and the Bears finished seventh.

It was back to second place for the Bears in 1926, trailing the Frankford Yellowjackets

Far right: A relaxed George Halas.

Yankees folded, but the Bears finished ninth with a 4-9-2 record; the Cardinals were fourth. This was the last year that Halas played for the Bears on the field.

Indeed, in 1930, Halas was no longer the coach of the Bears, letting Ralph Jones do the job. The Bears came in third and the Cardinals seventh, coached by the legendary Ernie Nevers.

The League was down to ten teams in 1931 and the Bears finished third and the Cardinals fourth. But the Bears won the championship in 1932 under Jones with Grange, Bronko Nagurski and Luke Johnsos on the team. The Cardinals ended up seventh in the eight-team league.

The league split into two divisions in 1933, with the Bears and Cardinals in the Western Division, along with the Portsmouth Spartans, the Green Bay Packers and the Cincinnati Reds. The Bears won the division after a playoff with the Green Bay Packers. The two teams finished tied for first place in the Western Division. Quarterbacked by Sid Luckman, the Bears spotted the Packers a 7-0 first-quarter lead, then used an 81-yard return by Hugh Gallarneau as the front end of 30 consecutive points en route to a 33-14 victory.

The Bears beat the winner of the Eastern Division, the New York Giants, 23-21 in the league championship game. Halas was back at the helm for this one. For their shares of this crucial game, the Bears' players received $210.34 and the Giants $140.22. And these

Above: Jay Berwanger (with the ball) playing for the University of Chicago in a Big Ten game against the University of Wisconsin. Berwanger was the first to win the Heisman Trophy as the best football player in the nation, and was never sorry that he turned down a chance to play professional football.

Opposite: The Chicago Bears (in white) play a game in Wrigley Field against the Brooklyn Dodgers – 1935.

Below: A publicity shot of 'Red' Grange with all 12 members of a girl's football team piled on top of him.

(by one game, because the Bears had three ties and the Yellowjackets only one). The Cardinals were tenth in the 22-team league. Grange wasn't with the Bears, having, with his manager, created the American Football League with Grange playing for the New York team. The American Football League vanished after one season.

In 1927 things had changed. Red Grange took his AFL team, the New York Yankees, into the National Football League and finished sixth in the 12-team league. The Bears were second to the New York Giants, and the Chicago Cardinals finished ninth.

There was a ten-team league in 1928, and the Bears were fifth and the Cardinals ninth, winning but one game. Red Grange was back with the Bears in 1929, after his New York

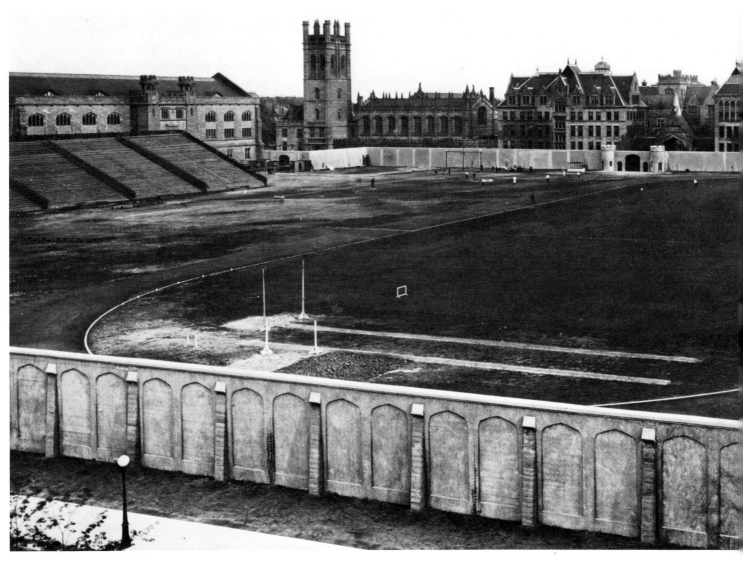

players played the whole 60 minutes in those days.

The Bears won their division championship in 1934 and the Cardinals pulled themselves up into fourth place. The New York Giants beat the Bears in the championship game, 30-13, in the famous 'sneaker game.' The temperature stood at 9° in New York on 9 December, and the Polo Grounds were covered with sheet ice to the point where no one could keep his footing. But in the second half, New York's coach, 'Stout' Steve Owens, provided his team with basketball shoes borrowed from a local college, and achieved four touchdowns and the rout of the Bears, who had beaten the Giants twice during the regular season.

The year 1935 was a disaster, as the Cardinals finished third and the Bears fourth in the by now four-team Western Division. But Douglas Russell of the Cardinals led the league in rushing with 499 yards, and another Cardinal, Bill Smith, tied for the league lead in kicking field goals with six. That year Red Grange retired.

Nineteen thirty-six was a little better, with the Bears finishing second and the Cardinals fourth. But it was that year that Jay Ber-wanger, the University of Chicago halfback and the first Heisman Trophy winner, was drafted first by the Philadelphia Eagles and turned them down. The Bears won their division in 1937, with the Cardinals finishing fourth out of the five teams, but the Bears lost the championship game to the Washington Redskins 28-21. The Bears were third and the Cardinals fifth in the five-team Western Division in 1938.

In 1939 the Bears climbed to second place behind Green Bay, while the Cardinals still wallowed in last place, winning only one game. In 1940 the Bears won the division and the Cardinals finished last, but at least they won two games.

The championship game that year between the Chicago Bears and the Washington Redskins was a historic one. Years later, when George Halas was asked what his greatest thrill in his long career had been, he smiled and said, '73-0.' There was no doubt what he meant. Professional athletic scores are usually forgotten the day after the game, but this one lives on.

The most fantastic exhibition of sheer football power and genius, combined with perfect timing and good luck, fashioned this cham-

Above: Stagg Field at the University of Chicago. Under the stands to the right, Enrico Fermi and the members of his Manhattan Project produced the first nuclear chain reaction (the fission of uranium isotope U-235) in 1942.

Opposite: Amos Alonzo Stagg (second from left), the long-time football coach at the University of Chicago, with three of his players from the national football champions of 1899 – Dr. Ralph Hamill, W S Kennedy and Jonathan Webb – on 9 November 1929.

pionship game into one that will be mentioned with awe as long as football is played. Washington was far from an outclassed team. In fact, their season record (9 and 2) was better than the Bears' (8 and 3). They were expected to win, especially since Sammy Baugh, their quarterback, was having his best year ever.

The Bears received the opening kickoff, and on the second play Bill Osmanski sped around his left end for 68 yards and a touchdown. Jack Manders converted. Sid Luckman, the Bear quarterback, scored the next touchdown with a one-yard plunge after driving the team 80 yards. Bob Snyder kicked the extra point. Joe Maniaci followed Osmanski's trail around left end for 42 yards and a touchdown, and Phil Matinovich made the conversion to make it 21-0 at the end of the first quarter.

The second quarter was fairly quiet. The only scoring was Luckman's 30-yard pass to Ken Kavanaugh in the end zone and Snyder's second conversion.

Hampton Pool intercepted a Sammy Baugh pass to open the second half and ran 19 yards for a touchdown, with Dick Plasman converting. Ray Nolting blasted for 23 yards and another score, and this time Plasman missed the conversion. George McAfee then intercepted Roy Zimmerman's pass and returned it 34 yards for a touchdown; Joe Stydahar kicked the extra point. Clyde 'Bulldog' Turner got into the act by intercepting

another Zimmerman throw and going 21 yards into the end zone. The Redskins blocked Maniaci's conversion attempt. This made it 54-0 as the third quarter ended.

Harry Clark went around his right end for 44 yards and a touchdown and Gary Famiglietti missed the conversion. A few minutes later, Famiglietti atoned for his mistake by smashing over from the two-yard line after Bulldog Turner had recovered Frankie Filchock's fumble. This time, Sollie Sherman passed to Maniaci for the extra point. Clark scored the final touchdown from the one-yard line, but the Sherman-Maniaci conversion pass went wild. The reason that they passed instead of kicking for the conversion late in the game was that they were running out of footballs because so many had been kicked into the stands and not returned. Ten different Bears had scored 11 touchdowns and six different Bears had scored seven conversions.

The Bears won their division again in 1941, with the Cardinals coming in in fourth place. This time the Bears beat the New York Giants by a mere 37-9 in the championship game.

Those were truly the Glamour Years in Chicago professional football. Featured were the Hall of Famers Guy Chamberlin (1921, Chicago Staleys, 1927, Chicago Cardinals), John 'Paddy' Driscoll (1920-25, Chicago Cardinals, 1926-9, Chicago Bears), Harold 'Red' Grange (1925, 1929-34, Chicago Bears), George Halas, Ed Healey (1922-7 Chicago Bears), Bill Hewitt (1932-6 Chicago Bears), Walt Kiesling (1929-33 Chicago Cardinals, 1934 Chicago Bears), Sid Luck-

man (1939–50 Chicago Bears), William 'Link' Lyman (1933–4 Chicago Bears), George McAfee (1940–41, 1945–50 Chicago Bears), George Musso (1933–4 Chicago Bears), Bronko Nagurski (1930–37 Chicago Bears), Ernie Nevers (1929–31 Chicago Cardinals), Joe Stydahar (1936–42, 1945–6, Chicago Bears), George Trafton (1921 Staleys, 1922–32, Chicago Bears) and Clyde 'Bulldog' Turner (1940–52, Chicago Bears).

The National Hockey League expanded from Canada down south to the United States in 1924. To the Boston Bruins went the league's first American franchise. The Pittsburgh Pirates, adopting the same name as the city's baseball team, won a franchise in 1925. That same year, yet another outfit – the New York Americans – took shape. Then, in 1926, the league added three more teams – the New York Rangers, the Chicago Black Hawks and the Detroit Cougars (later to be rechristened the Red Wings).

Until reaching their glory years in the late 1960s, the Chicago Black Hawks wrote one of the oddest pages in the history of the

National Hockey League. The team came into being when a wealthy Chicago sportsman, Major Frederic McLaughlin, purchased the Portland (Oregon) Rosebuds from Lester Patrick's financially troubled Western League for $100,000, and renamed the team in honor of his World War I Army Division. With Pete Muldoon coaching, and with four major stars in the lineup – wingman Babe Dye, forward James (Dick) Irvin, wingman George Hay and goalkeeper Hugh Lehman – the Hawks worked their way up to the American Division's third place in their maiden season, with Irvin placing second in league scoring, right behind the champion, Bill Cook of the New York Rangers. But except for a year here and there, the Glamour Years were marked by one disaster after another.

There is little doubt that many of the team's problems stemmed directly from owner McLaughlin, a man with little hockey experience but an abundance of impatience. These two factors drove him to hire what seemed to be an unending succession of

Opposite top: The Chicago Stadium, home of the Black Hawks, in 1929. At that time it was the largest indoor sports arena in the world.

Below: The Chicago Black Hawk team of 1926 – their first year in the National Hockey League.

Above: Pete Muldoon, the manager of the Black Hawks in 1926.

writer's fancy on a day when good copy was not to be had, the curse was supposedly handed out by Pete Muldoon on the occasion of his firing. The deposed coach reportedly had intoned: 'The Black Hawks will never finish first,' and then continued (so the legend goes) to repeat it through the coming years. Whether by coincidence or by psychic force, the team lived up to the hex. It did not finish at the top of its division for four decades.

And, whether by coincidence or psychic force, there is no denying that the Hawks did suffer more than their fair share of misfortune in their early seasons, with one of the worst being the 1927–8 campaign. For openers, Babe Dye broke his leg in a pre-season practice session and, because of the injury and the fact that he was nearing the end of his career, was sent to the New York Americans; he posted a disappointing season there, retired, entered the construction business, and lived in Chicago until his death in 1962.

Next, goalkeeper Hugh Lehman turned 40 during the 1927–8 season and found that he could no longer handle the physical strains that went with his job. After leading the league in ice time in 1926–7 (2797 minutes) he played but 250 minutes and retired.

Putting the frosting on this cake of misfortune was Dick Irvin's injury. During a game in Montreal, he crashed into the Maroon's defenseman Mervyn (Red) Dutton,

coaches over the years. He dropped Muldoon after a successful first season and then fired Muldoon's replacement – Barney Stanley – before the man was able to complete a full season. Dick Irvin, with his playing days over because of an injury, took on the coaching job in 1928 and hung on until the end of the 1929–30 season. In 1931–2 the team enjoyed the services of two coaches. The 1932–3 outing posted a coaching record – three. By the time that the Hawks took their first Stanley Cup at the close of the 1938–9 season, they had worked under no fewer than 10 coaches. After the Cup win, Coach Tommy Gorman was released and Bill Stewart took his place.

But the club's headaches went beyond McLaughlin's revolving door policy for coaches. Despite the presence of Dye, Irvin and company in the initial lineup, McLaughlin had the habit of choosing players who, while of professional caliber, were simply not up to the league's competition.

On top of all else, there was the fact that the Black Hawks gave every indication of being a bad-luck franchise, with many fans saying that this was the result of the 'Muldoon Curse.' A legend that may have been a sports

hit the ice and lay there with a fractured skull. On recovering after a hospitalization of several weeks, Irvin was refused permission to play for the remainder of the season by a concerned Frank Calder, the league president. He came back for the 1928–9 competition, participated for a few games, and then was appointed coach. It marked the beginning of one of the more illustrious coaching careers in the history of professional hockey.

But it must be said that the Black Hawks' early years did not consist only of bad luck and the fruits of an erratic management. There were two developments that ran contrary to the team's history in those days. First, during Irvin's tenure as coach, McLaughlin ordered the use of rapid line changes, bringing in fresh troops whenever a line seemed to tire. The idea was based on a theory that McLaughlin had learned in the army – that fresh troops always have the edge over a fatigued enemy. It was a strategy that has since become basic to the game.

Second, in sharp contrast to the team's usual hiring practices, McLaughlin brought in Charlie Gardiner to replace goalkeeper Lehman. Gardiner looked to be anything but a star during his first four performances, but then did a sudden about-face and went on to become one of the finest goaltenders ever seen in the National Hockey League. He played for only seven years, his career ending tragically in 1935 when he died soon after undergoing brain surgery. But in those seven years, he produced 42 shutouts, posted a splendid record of 2.13 goals-against average and won the Vezina Award (for best goalie) in 1931–2 and 1933–4. Gardiner was named to the league's All-Star first team in 1931, 1932 and 1934, and to the second team in 1933. His appearance in the Hawks' 1933–4 Stanley Cup victory has long ranged high among the most courageous performances ever seen in National Hockey League play.

The 1933–4 Cup competition saw the Black Hawks down the Montreal Canadiens in the quarter-final round and then move to the championship series by defeating the Montreal Maroons in the semi-finals. The Chicagoans took the championship series, 3 games to 1 over the Detroit Red Wings. Four years later, at the close of the 1937–38 season, the Black Hawks earned their second Cup by handing the Toronto Maple Leafs a 3-games-to-1 defeat after beating the Canadiens in the quarters-finals and the New York Americans in the semifinals.

In the wake of the successful 1937–8 campaign, the Black Hawks suffered such a poor season that the fans stayed away in droves. The club, in fact, had come to the threshold of a two-decade period of failure that would make the problems of the earlier years seem as nothing.

Below: Black Hawks Couture, Trudell and Gottselig – 1933.

POSTLUDE

Just before the United States entered World War II, the America First Committee, headed by Sears, Roebuck's president, General Robert E Wood, campaigned for isolationism. The *Chicago Tribune* published editorials against war, claiming that the paper's statewide poll showed that 74 percent of those questioned believed America should stay out of the fighting. Of course, because of the paper's isolationistic stance, many people did not believe the results, and Robert Maynard Hutchins, the youthful president of the University of Chicago, commissioned a poll of his own. He found out that the *Tribune* was right – 74.7 percent of the people in the state were opposed to the war.

With the war heightening in Europe, the isolationists in Chicago brought America's hero, Colonel Charles A Lindbergh, to Soldier Field on 4 August 1940. He gave a speech to 40,000 people, telling them that the United States was in trouble if the government forced them into a fight that was none of their business. But the draft was on and men of military age were still registering and being inducted into the peacetime Armed Forces.

Interventionists hated the reactionary *Chicago Tribune*, and were delighted to learn that Marshall Field was planning to begin publishing an alternative morning newspaper. Indeed, a contest was run to determine the name for the new tabloid-size paper. One wag suggested the *Chicago Truth*, explaining that when people went to buy their morning paper, the newsdealer would say, 'What do you want, the *Truth* or the *Tribune*?' Finally

named the Chicago *Sun*, the paper first appeared on 4 December 1941, selling 896,000 copies the first day and challenging the *Tribune* for the morning market in the city.

Three days later the Japanese attacked Pearl Harbor.

After Pearl Harbor, Chicagoans gave whole-hearted support to the war effort. The city set a record by spending $1.3 billion for war plants. The Stevens Hotel was requisitioned as a training center and barracks for servicemen. The Chicago Beach Hotel became a military hospital. The Auditorium Theater became a servicemen's recreation center, with bowling alleys where its stage used to be.

The Chicago anti-war committees closed up shop, Hitler's picture disappeared from the Milwaukee Avenue saloons, and the Glamour Years were over.

Opposite: Charles and Anne Morrow Lindbergh shortly after their marriage. It was Lindbergh for whom Chicago named its famous beacon, and it was Lindbergh who urged Chicagoans to stay out of the war in Europe.

Below left: The Stevens Hotel (now the Conrad Hilton) on Michigan Avenue was turned into a training center when America entered World War II.

Below: Phil Cavaretta, who was to become a star for the Chicago Cubs.

INDEX

Acknowledgements
The authors and publisher would like to thank the following people who have helped in the preparation of this book: David Eldred, who designed it; Robin Langley Sommer, who edited it; Mary R Raho who did the picture research; and Cynthia Klein, who prepared the index.

Picture Credits
Courtesy of The Art Institute of Chicago: 77 (Ivan Albright, Self-Portrait at East Division Street), 65 (Alson Skinner Clark, Coffee Shop).
Bettmann Archive: 2–3, 6, 7, 8, 9, 10, 12–13, 14, 15 (top), 16, 17, 18, 19, 20 (top), 22, 23, 24, 28, 29, 30, 31, 32–33, 34 (bottom), 35, 36 (bottom), 37 (top), 39 (bottom), 42, 43, 44, 45, 46, 47, 48, 49, 50, 51 (top), 52, 54–55, 56, 57, 58, 60, 61, 62, 63, 64, 76 (bottom), 81, 82, 83, 84, 86, 87, 88, 89, 90–91, 92, 93, 94 (left), 95, 96, 97, 98–99, 100, 101, 102 (right), 103, 104 (bottom), 105, 106, 107, 108–109, 110 (right), 111 (top), 113, 114, 115 (top), 116–117, 119, 120, 121 (top left and bottom), 122–123, 126 (bottom), 127, 128–129, 131 (top), 132, 133, 134, 135, 136 (bottom), 137, 141, 142–143, 143, 144, 146–147, 149, 150, 151, 152, 153, 155 (bottom), 156, 158 (bottom), 159, 160 (bottom), 162, 163, 164 (top), 165 (bottom), 166 (bottom), 167 (bottom), 168, 169, 172, 176 (top), 178 (top), 179 (top), 180, 181, 183, 184, 185, 186, 188 (left), 189.
Bison Picture Library: 1, 26, 69 (top and bottom left, bottom right), 72 (top and bottom right), 136 (top).
Cadillac: 73 (top right).
Chicago Bears: 179 (bottom).
Chicago Historical Society: 15 (bottom), 20 (bottom), 21, 25, 27, 34 (top), 36 (top), 37 (bottom), 38, 39 (top), 51 (bottom), 52, 66, 67, 68, 70, 71, 72 (top left), 74, 75, 76 (top), 79, 80, 85, 94–95, 102 (left), 104 (top), 110 (left), 111 (bottom), 112, 115 (bottom), 118, 121 (top right), 122, 123, 124, 125, 130, 131 (bottom), 142, 145, 148, 154, 155 (top), 157, 158 (top), 160 (top), 161, 164 (bottom), 165 (top), 166 (top), 167 (top), 173, 182–183, 186–187.
Chrysler Corp.: 73 (top left).
Country Music Foundation: 137 (top), 138, 139.
Ford Motor Company: 73 (bottom right).
TPS/Fox Photos: 126 (top).
Library of Congress: 40–41, 157 (bottom).
National Baseball Library, Cooperstown, New York: 78 (all 4), 170–171, 174, 175, 176 (bottom), 177, 178 (bottom) 188 (right).
Pacific Mills: 73 (bottom left).
RCA: 72 (bottom left).
Courtesy VOGUE: 69 (top right), copyright (c) 1926 (renewed) 1954, 1982 by the Condé Nast Publications Inc.